THE GRAND DESIGN—V
Reflections of a soul/oversoul

By the same author

THE GRAND DESIGN — I
Reflections of a soul/oversoul

THE GRAND DESIGN — II
Reflections of a soul/oversoul

THE GRAND DESIGN — III
Reflections of a soul/oversoul

THE GRAND DESIGN — IV
Reflections of a soul/oversoul

THE GRAND DESIGN
Selected Excerpts

A FREE SPIRIT

LIVING WITHOUT FEAR

THE GRAND DESIGN—V

Reflections of a soul/oversoul

by

Patrick Francis

Website:
www.geocities.com/granddesignie

Auricle Enterprises

Auricle Enterprises
30 Old Court Manor
Firhouse
Dublin 24
Tel. (01) 4523793

ISBN 0-9525509 4 6

Typessetting by STF, Celbridge, Co. Kildare, Ireland.
Printed by ColourBooks, Baldoyle, Dublin 13, Ireland.

Contents

Preface

In the preface to the third book in this series I mentioned that I wasn't sure how many volumes there would be altogether but that I felt there would be at least five. This is the fifth and I now know that it's the last book in the series.

Some readers may have begun to wonder why wasn't all the material put into one book rather than being fragmented into several, which maybe makes it more difficult to read one volume without referring to one or more of the others. As mentioned in the final chapter of this book, one of the reasons was to create a feeling of continuity. It seems to me too that I wouldn't have been ready for several reasons (including financial, which I'll go into later) to process the whole lot together, that I needed to expand my consciousness before I could absorb and communicate in a comprehensible way what was coming through to me. Also, perhaps the type of material in the books is more easily absorbed in relatively small doses.

Because, of course, it is desirable that as far as possible each book can be read on its own without reference to the others — for myself, I don't like having to interrupt the flow of reading in order to refer to earlier material or to footnotes — some repetition from book to book has been unavoidable. It has been kept to a minimum, I hope, and done with the aim of reinforcing and/or expanding earlier material.

I often look back with wonder at what has transpired since I —

unwittingly — started writing the first book in October, 1981. So much heady excitement and doubts were all mixed up together. How could it be that such an apparently highly evolved being would see fit to communicate with me? And what sort of a name was Shebaka? I liked the sound of it and its very unfamiliarity made it more credible to me, but was I going to be the recipient of some esoteric Eastern philosophy? What would people make of it all — that's if I ever plucked up enough courage to reveal it?

Before I haltingly embarked on the public presentation of the communications I was told that they would ultimately spread throughout the world. I found it impossible to envisage how that would happen — in my darker moments I wondered was I just told that as a sop to encourage me to go on with the books — and for quite a long time after the first book was published it seemed most unlikely that the prediction would be borne out. Yet already it has been — admittedly in a very limited way, quantity wise, so far. (An exciting development this year was the publication of the first book in German; what was particularly encouraging about the develop- ment was that it came "out of the blue" as far as I was concerned without any initiative on my part.) That's one of the reasons why I often say to people not to set limits according to what they can envisage from where they are at any particular time. In my experi- ence things always turn out better than seems possible if we allow ourselves to trust enough.

Now that the series of books is complete perhaps it would be helpful if I summarise briefly what I think they're about.

The first book presents an overview of life and seeks to provide answers to age-old questions, such as, where do we come from?; where are we going?; is life just a haphazard occurrence or is there more to it than being born, existing for a certain number of hours, days, months or years?; is there a Source?; if so, who or what is it?; what's our relation- ship with it?; if there is life after death what's it like?; are there such places as Heaven and Hell?; are there angels, devils?; is reincarnation a possibility?; where does non-human life (animals, etc.) fit into the over- all scheme of things?; who or what are we at all?

The subsequent books expand on what's contained in the first book and introduce much more additional material, all aimed at increasing our understanding of life and helping our growth in awareness so that ideally we free ourselves from whatever our accumulation of negative karmic effects happens to be.

The last two books, in particular, explore how life in spirit can be mirrored by life on earth with fairly detailed suggestions as to how that can be done.

A constant theme running through all the books is that we are all spirit beings who happen to be on a human journey for a little while, that we lost awareness of our own divinity and are seeking to regain it, and that we have guides/guardian angels to help us to do so, which includes helping us in our day to day living with all its practical issues.

For nearly fifteen years, even though there have been considerable time gaps between some of the communications, I have lived with these books. There have been many other things going on in my life, of course, — some of them traumatic — but always the books have been continuing to declare their presence. Now that the series is finished I'm feeling a bit desolate. I began to wonder (just a little!) whether it's time for me to move on — or off the planet, in other words. I'd like to continue writing, though, as well as with other areas of my life which are a source of much joy and privileged interaction with many wonderful people, so I'll have to "wait and see". Since I got into whatever it is that I'm into (I don't want to put labels on it) I don't tend to bother much with plans. Life unfolds and then there's more wonder in it. I don't always remember to follow the suggestions given in the books but generally I do and I must say that, in my experience, they make great sense; if that wasn't so I don't suppose I'd have been happy about the books being published. I hasten to add, though, that the fact that they make sense to me doesn't mean that I expect that to be so for anybody else; I'm delighted when it is, needless to say.

Over the years I have received lovely letters from many people who have found the books helpful. I have been told repeatedly by different people that reading the books has seemed like a reminder to them of things they already knew but hadn't consciously realised; for me that has been very affirming. I'm very grateful to all those people and I hope that those who have written to me and haven't received replies will forgive me. I like writing but for some reason I find it hard to get down to writing letters. No excuse, I know!

To give the full picture I need to say, too, that some people have told me that they found one or other of the books heavy going.

When I was writing the third book I included a personal interjection about Wendy, a lovely tabby cat. I referred in it to the thoughtfulness of a veterinary surgeon. I didn't name him then in case that would have been an interference with his privacy. Subsequently he suffered a severe illness and died earlier this year. He was a wonderful man. I'm sure that since his transition he has had hordes of animals lining up to thank him for all the loving healing he so unstintingly gave them. His name was Colm Rafter.

One of the reasons why I included in this book a chapter entitled *Personal Interlude* was that people often ask me about my communication with Shebaka and I wanted to show it in action, in a manner of speaking, and also to suggest it as a way that readers who are interested might like to try for themselves with their own guides. Questions such as "is it real?" or "am I talking to myself?" will be intruding, of course, but that's inevitable, given that the communication has to come through a person's inner processes. A useful barometer is whether the material in the communications feels authentic and makes sense.

The format of this book is somewhat different from that of the others in that a significant proportion of it employs dialogue rather than straightforward discourse. Again, this is done deliberately in order to remove any aura of mystique and to show the process of communication in a more obviously interactive way.

In the chapter entitled *Adventure in Spirit* the blank spaces are intended to convey passage of time, which is probably obvious, but I thought I'd mention it anyway. No suggestions are included about periods of time because they would be variable depending on whatever was appropriate for the individual adventurer. While we're human we can't dispense with time even when we take a trip into timelessness!

At first, when conscious communication with guides became a feature for me, I thought that I'd never again have any hassle or difficulty in my life. For example, when it became clear that the writing which I was doing as a result of my communication with Shebaka was taking book form, and after I had got over my reluctance to publish — a reluctance which I have to confess was due mainly to my nervousness about what it would do to my "image",- I thought that all I had to do was to submit the manuscript to a publisher and there would be automatic acceptance and after perhaps a little time (not too much!) the people for whom the material was intended would find it. The reality was much more prosaic.

Even though I wasn't using my full name (I dropped my surname, whch is McMahon, for reasons which I outlined in the preface to the second book) I wasn't keen to try a local publisher so I sent the manuscript to an English firm. It was returned to me with a note saying that their lists were closed. I tried another English company, with a similar outcome. I sent it to an American publisher, too, but with no success — I didn't even get the manuscript back. I went through a period of wondering then whether my lack of success in finding a publisher was "a sign" that the manuscript wasn't intended to be published at all. Even though I felt rejected and disappointed there was also a sneaking relief that maybe I was being let "off the hook".

Some time later — I can't remember precisely the sequence of events — I came across a spiritual type book which was published by the Regency Press in London, so I decided to try that firm. Without much delay I received a very nice letter from the manager of the firm saying that they would like to publish the book but that the nature of their operation was such that they could only do so on a cost sharing basis.

I was now presented with a neat dilemma. I could get the book published but to do so I'd have to pay what was to me a considerable sum of money — which I hadn't got anyway. There was also the point that having the book published in that way wouldn't be the same as if it had the recognition of being accepted as being worthy of publication in its own right; in other words, by paying for its publication I felt I wouldn't have any objective evaluation of it as a book.

I let the matter rest for some time — but it wouldn't stay asleep! I eventually decided that I was being asked to demonstrate my faith in the philosophy presented in the book. I borrowed the money, at the then exorbitant rates of interest, and the first book made its public appearance in due course.

Now that the book was out — and it was thrilling to see it in its final form — I felt I had done my bit and that it didn't need any more effort from me. Helped by some good reviews in English publications the book began to circulate, but when the first edition was nearly sold out the publishers decided that sales had been too slow to justify reprinting. Another dilemma! Was that it, the end, then?

In spite of my unwillingness to undertake any publicity, I didn't want to let the book go out of print. I wrote to the manager of the Regency Press to say that I would guarantee to buy any copies not sold within a time scale of, I think, eight months if they would reprint. He obligingly agreed to do so and the book continued to live. (I'd like to take this opportunity to express my gratitude to the manager of the Regency Press, John Thorpe, for his unfailing kindness, consideration and encouragement to me at all times. He provided the platform without which I mightn't have had the impetus to keep going. While, because of further developments which I won't go into now, I didn't continue to publish with the Regency Press after the second book, they still act as international agents for all the books.)

At some stage a kind friend, whom I had met originally in the course of my official work, asked me would I like him to do some marketing of the book. Conscious of the guarantee which I had given to the Regency Press, I was glad to accept his offer. He was (is) an experienced communicator. In what seemed to me a miraculously short space of time he had arranged with several major bookshops, as well as other more specialised ones, that they would carry the book. He also torpedoed me on to a national radio programme. The book thus began to find an established niche and has to date been reprinted four times. The guarantee became irrelevant — providentially!

The other volumes followed.

I decided to record my experience in getting the first book off the ground in the hope that it might be helpful to any readers who may find themselves seemingly blocked by obstacles in the way of getting where they want to go, or who may feel that they have been abandoned by their guides. As I understand the process, the help that we get from guides often operates by way of providing opportunities for us to step into what was for us hitherto unknown territory; in other words, if we take a chance and put a toe in the water, we'll get all the support we need. We're invited to trust and to put that trust into action. In 'going with the flow' we may find ourselves catapulted out of hitherto safe, settled ways of life into what may sometimes seem like chaos, at least for awhile. But that's how shifts in consciousness happen.

In writing the books I have condensed a lot of often weighty material into what I hope is a simple format of words. It may be a failing of mine — I don't know — but I don't like to overuse words; I think their meaning gets clouded when they are indiscriminately scattered. Anyway I have done my best with them.

In earlier prefaces I have apologised for the use of 'he' where 'he/she' would be more appropriate. In this book I deliberately tried to get myself into situations where I wouldn't have to use either. I couldn't escape completely, but I don't think any reader will be too exasperated this time if she finds 'he' where 'she' should be as well; I hope not anyway.

Thanks very much for your company and encouragement. And I suppose I should say thanks to Shebaka, too!

Patrick Francis

July 1996

The calamity of human ignorance

8th March 1995: Once again we embark on a new venture even before the previous one has found its public voice. As I intimated when we began (in 1981) what has evolved to be this continuing series of books, I'm always only a thought away from you, although you often find it difficult to feel the connection. My communication with you has to be unobtrusive as this is a collaborative effort rather than a directive one; in other words, I'm not presuming to tell you how, or what, to write, but I am, as it were, shining a light in front of you as we travel along the path of illumination.

I welcome the readers who have shared our explorations with us and I hope that they will find what we communicate in this book enlightening and helpful. As ever, my love and the love of those who are joined with me in spirit on this project surrounds and protects you all.

In our decision to discuss in this session what a soul (in spirit) described to you as the calamity of human ignorance I wouldn't like to convey an impression that souls in spirit have all the answers; indeed they don't — but they have access to them as they regain their lost awareness. According as souls who are going through a human experience find ways of lifting and letting go the veils of illusion, physical death will become a celebratory homecoming rather than a source of distress and confusion and devastating separation which, unfortunately, it often is.

When one looks at the history of humanity it's easy to see how calamity can be an apt description. All through the ages people have sought to impose their views, their will, their way of life, on others, sometimes by force, sometimes by laws, sometimes as the self-appointed representatives of a supreme being, inevitably by fear. Many people have done so, and continue to do so, in order to gain positions of control or influence, and that, at least, however deplorable, is straightforward. The real tragedy is where people genuinely and sincerely believe that they, and only they, know "the truth" and want to make sure that everybody else lives by that truth. That's the most dangerous and calamitous ignorance of all and can be testified to as such by the multitudes who have been victims of it. I classify it as the worst type of ignorance because it is so insidious, judgemental and arrogant in its righteousness.

There is only one truth — God. There's only one true God. These are the sort of factual statements which, without elaboration, contribute to the spread of ignorance because of people's tendencies, albeit understandable, towards confining God within the structures of rigid belief systems controlled by conditioning. However, when it is accepted that God is all and all is contained in God and nothing has ever existed, exists, or will exist, outside of God, it can be seen that there's an infinity of aspects or attributes or, dare I say, truths, in God. For example, each human being is an expression of God in a way that's unique to that person. It's impossible to define God; therefore it's impossible to define truth. Anybody that says he knows the mind of God, that he knows truth, is deluding himself. That's why, ultimately, there can never be any absolutes of right or wrong, good or bad. Absolutes only exist through definition and definition involves limitation. A person may believe that he knows himself but then something happens through which he reveals himself to himself in a new light; and so the process of revelation continues. People live by their perceptions which are usually determined by their conditioning. If they are open-minded their perceptions change as their awareness increases. That's the wonder of ever-unfolding consciousness; it's never confined within dogmatic belief systems, it lays down no laws, and sets no limits; it respects the freedom of every individual to live his life in whatever way his expression of God is manifesting at any particular time.

In the long run, it's more dogmatism than ignorance that's the calamity — although, of course, dogmatism is a product of ignorance.

Utopia?

3rd May: In our last book we discussed utopia in terms of a small country of about four million people. During your recent visit to the United States of America you wondered how could the blueprint work in such a vast continent and even, for example, in such a huge city as New York. Is it conceivable that the enormous range of essential services could be organised without extensive hierarchical structures to administer them?

From a purely material standpoint the scale of what has been achieved in the United States in such a relatively short period of time is awe-inspiring; it illustrates clearly the creative potential in people when they have the scope to express it.

If I may use an illustration which may initially seem inappropriate but yet is very relevant, I ask you to imagine the magnitude of America, its towering skyscrapers, its seemingly never-ending motorways, its sheer breathtaking magnificence, and add in all the other continents which complete planet earth, with all their diversities and complexities and immensities and, also, take into account all the other planets, of which you know relatively little other than that they're quite large(!), and you still haven't got an impression, even to the extent of the tiniest fraction, of the capacity of one soul, not to mention the infinity of God. All the same, you have a strong indication of what souls can do when they are united in a common purpose. Any community, any country, any continent, no matter how large, is a collection of individual souls. As they cooperate in expansion of consciousness anything is possible. Human beings have shown in many ways, often regrettably, destructive ones, what they can achieve. As they grow in increasing awareness of their divinity there are no limits to what is achievable even within the human state.

Soul mates

3rd June: You have been asked for some elaboration on the subject of soul mates as presented in the session on special relationships in our last book. Specifically, the question raised is whether each soul (oversoul) has just one soul mate or is it possible that a soul may have a number of soul mates.

By exercising their free will in ways which caused increasing diminution of their awareness (as outlined in our first book) souls placed themselves in states of limitation. As a result, their ways of relating to each other became extremely confused. Thus, in the human condition there have been all sorts of conflicts, cruelties, misunderstandings. People's abilities to reach levels of intimacy with each other became blocked by fear in its many forms. Yet, sooner or later, each person needs to be able to feel the freedom of revealing himself totally as he is, in an unconditionally loving way, to at least one special other person. And, as he regains his awareness, each person will inevitably find that special other person while they are still in human form.

Because of the vulnerability imposed by conditioning people have, understandably, hidden behind defensive, protective masks, which have enabled them to relate to each other and the world around them while keeping their thoughts to themselves if they wish to do so. This can work in the human state due to the density of the earth vibration. In spirit, however, because of the lightness of vibration, it's not possible to hide one's feelings or thoughts. If a person hasn't found the security of being able to reveal himself while he is still on earth, he's bound to find adjustment to the spirit (non-physical) state more difficult since his mask is no longer operable. If, on the other hand, a person has broken the ice by reaching an ease of self-revelation, even if only with one other person, that will have opened the door to his being more comfortable with the process in a more general way, which, in turn, will make his adjustment to the spirit state easier.

An intimate relationship does not necessarily need sexual expression or may not have any sexual overtones except in the sense that the people involved may be of the same, or different, genders. By soul mates I mean two souls who relate to each other — or, commune with each other may be a more accurate way of putting it, — in a totally intimate way without feeling a need to keep any part of themselves in reserve.

In spirit, in its ultimate state of full awareness, there are no limitations. It follows that every soul (oversoul) can have all the soul mates it chooses to have. While a soul is going through its earth journey it's a considerable achievement if it finds one.

Personal interlude

5th–29th June: **Patrick Francis** Since we commenced our communication in a more conscious way in 1981 four books have been published. While, of course, I accept the validity and the reality of the communications or I wouldn't have allowed the books to be published, yet sometimes I wish I could establish a more obvious — to me — link. Is there something more I can do to achieve that end?

Shebaka As I informed you at the start of our explorations, I am available to connect with you whenever suits you. Because we have been endeavouring to present in simple form concepts and ideas which are often complex, this cannot be done in an off-hand way — in other words, in a way which is incidental to your other activities. I don't have to concern myself with conserving my energy, but you do, because you are a human being not immune, if I may be somewhat flippant, from the creeping effects of the passing,and seemingly tantalisingly shorter, years. It's not open to me to write the books — that's your chosen role — or to provide you with a language structure to express our communication; you are the physical agent, with all that that implies. We function in cooperation in accordance with the utopian way, which means that however you approach your role is fine with me.

But since you ask how can you achieve a more obvious link with me I can only suggest that you (a) rearrange your priorities so that you can devote more time to our communication when your energy levels are at their highest, and (b) set a regular pattern whereby our communication can take place, ideally on a daily basis, in a relaxed manner.

PF The way things are this year I don't think I can do much more than I'm already doing to implement your suggestions.

Since you can see without limitation, and I can't, the broad design of where we're going with our cooperative venture (although I understand the utopian concept) would you please help me with how best I can manage next year — in a general sense I mean, of course.

S You will recall that one of our earliest sessions in what became our first book was about simplicity. Life in spirit at what I have called the fourth stage and beyond that is totally simple, whereas, as you know, a feature of human existence is how complicated it is. So the fundamental question to examine is — how do you make your life more simple? Leaving aside, just for the moment, all restrictions — duties, responsibilities, financial matters — what do you really want to do?

PF Writing and what follows from it, which would include talking to people about the material in the books.

S Then, if you want to make your life more simple, writing has to be given priority.

PF But now I have to bring the down-to-earth matters back into consideration. My dilemma is that my financial obligations are too heavy to allow me to concentrate my energies on writing which, based on my experience to date, has limited income-producing potential, at least in the short term.

S Where's your faith? Your trust? Isn't the abundance of the universe open to you?

What will happen, of course, is that, once you give writing a primary place in your life, more energy will be generated around the books and bring them to a wider readership. International avenues are opening up for them and, in general, the time has come for you — for yourself — to give them the acknowledgment they deserve.

Your financial needs will be met.

PF   Thanks. I'll let this year run and redesign next year to give priority to writing.

How to be successful?

11th July 1995–5th January 1996: A common source of pressure amongst human beings is to be accepted, and to accept themselves, as successes rather than failures. If that's so, it's reasonable to assume that there are general perceptions as to what constitutes success or failure. What are those perceptions?

Success is generally equated with, for example, material possessions, power, status, notable achievement, recognition of talent, fame, family security, sexual attractiveness, lovableness; while failure would encompass the lack of some or all of those.

When we consider how the spiritual and physical worlds can be increasingly integrated, perceptions of success and failure can bring us into diametrically opposed territories. It is, I suppose, obvious that somebody who amasses a considerable fortune through, say, entrepreneurial abilities may achieve widespread recognition on that account, but, when he comes to the end of his physical life, may find that he hasn't advanced, or may even have regressed, in spiritual terms. A person who lives a life of total obscurity may achieve far greater spiritual growth than one who becomes a celebrity; but the reverse may also be so. Choosing to reject participation in the world of commerce may be no greater guarantee of spiritual growth than opting to immerse oneself in that world.

The question posed in this session is — how to be successful? Implicit in that question is, of course, success in spiritual terms. Any reader who has been with us so far would, I'm sure, find any other interpretation somewhat surprising!

Because all human endeavour is expressed in stages and in a linear way, since you live within a time structure, it will be helpful, I hope, to set out, as follows, ingredients which, in my view, are essential towards the achievement of success:

1 Open-mindedness and tolerance: All human beings, without exception, are limited in their thinking by environmental, cultural, religious, ancestral influences. It is most important to acknowledge that, so that you no longer restrict yourself by taking up immediate and often fixed positions, which are inevitably controlled by your own experience. This doesn't mean that you stop yourself from expressing opinions; what it does mean is that you allow that your opinions are just your way for the present of looking at whatever comes within the ambit of your day to day existence; it also means that you accept without reservation the validity, from their point of view, of all others' ways of expression and that you do not attempt to manipulate or control how they express themselves. This doesn't imply that you won't help people, as best you can, to find their way; rather you will always allow them, unreservedly, freedom of choice.

2 Flexibility: In your day to day life you have, of course, to organise and plan; for example, the clothes you're going to wear, what you're going to eat, how you're going to allocate your time. Because you live in a physical world you have no choice, no matter how nonconformist you may be, but to deal with structures of time and space and the society in which you happen to be. It is understandable, then, that you may settle into fixed patterns of thinking and behaviour, and that any change in that pattern is disturbing for you. But the way of spirit is ever fluid, so that, if your life on earth is to fulfil its purpose, you need to be able to flow freely with change. If you're not flexible, you'll find, inevitably, that you're going to be faced with changes on a recurring basis until you reach a level of adaptability.

3 Creativity: Everybody, without exception, is creative, but most people don't believe that they are, and have never found ways of expressing their full creative potential. That's understandable because so many people are on the edge of survival struggling to have the minimal necessities, such as food and shelter, for the continuation of physical life. But yet it is true that the way people feel and think sets up a vibration which affects positively or negatively the conditions under which they live. In spiritual terms creativity means how souls feel and think. For a soul in spirit that's very obvious because the results are immediate. But the human being caught in a linear time frame and physical structure needs patience to see the effects of how he feels and thinks.

For example, a soul in spirit wishes to have a particular type of house and the house manifests immediately without any prohibitive, e.g., financial, complications. But for the human the wish is only the beginning of a long and detailed process until the house becomes a reality. Partners in a relationship, say, are likely to be faced with a heavy mortgage repayable over a lengthy period of time. Suppose they find themselves in a situation where they have been unable to pay arrears of the mortgage debt and are threatened with repossession of the family home, which will have the effect of leaving them and their children homeless. In their view, no amount of creative thinking. e.g., imagining the manifestation of the money needed to solve their problem, will change the dire situation they're in; so, as time goes on, they are more and more locked into a negative way of being where they will always be victims of circumstances, which, they feel, are outside of their control. Yet it is undoubtedly a fact that, even though on the face of it their situation is totally restrictive, the power to change it positively lies within themselves, in how they feel and think. Once they accept that they are continually creating their own destiny and take total responsibility for themselves, solutions will *always* present themselves; it's the constant, undeviating, way of the universe; it cannot be otherwise.

How can you fulfil your creative potential? So as not to make this session too cumbersome, I propose to explore that question separately later.

4   Truth: What I mean is being true to yourself. No matter how you try, you cannot relate to any two people in the same way; for each of them there will be shades of difference in your appearance, in what you say, in what you do, in how you are, even in your silences. So there's no point in trying to establish an image of how you think you ought to be, or how you think a person, or people generally, expect you to be. The statement to the effect that nobody can serve God and Mammon has, in my view, generally been completely misinterpreted; what it means is that nobody can be at one with God in him and at the same time serve a self-imposed image of what he thinks is expected of him by another and/or others. It is an essential ingredient in success that you present yourself to the world as you really are and let the world react in whatever way it will. That's not easy; but, if you're patient and tolerant with yourself, it will eventually become easier.

Being true to yourself doesn't mean that you have to reveal your all to everybody in your life or to make your views known at every available opportunity; it simply means that you're free to be whatever way you want to be, in how you are in yourself, how you feel and think, while, of course, always respecting others' truths.

5 Letting go: It is, of course, implicit in being true to yourself that you let go of egotism, i.e., the fearful, insecure, little "i". As you know, when I talk about letting go, I don't mean letting go of, or out of, but, rather, letting go into, i.e., into the greater "I", the divine "I". How can you do that? By (a) accepting that you are divine, that you are in God and God is in you; (b) also accepting that, as you are at present manifesting, you are revealing only an aspect of you as oversoul (I have explained in earlier sessions what I mean by oversoul); and (c) aligning yourself (ideally, in conscious cooperation with your guides) with your own divinity, with God in you and with God in all there is.

A central question in all this is — how can you align yourself with something you don't know? All your conditioning prepares you to move from the known to the known, so that you will invariably make a judgement on the basis of your own experience or knowledge as to how you will proceed in any given situation. Security for you tends to lie in being able to make an analysis fit into the box of your understanding and, of course, all boxes are structured and defined — and limited. So, you're at a loss, operating within limitation, when you consider God. You cannot define God, analyse God, or *know* God, so it is impossible for you to align yourself with God through your thinking, analytical processes. You need to go beyond thought. Where does that lead you? All that's beyond thought is feeling. You can feel God — in all sorts of ways (such as those we have previously outlined in the session on imagination in our last book), but, ultimately, in how you love. Once you love unconditionally you are one with your own divinity and with God in you and in all. You are then unlimited because you set no limits, and you have truly let go *into* rather than *out* of.

6   How do you know whether you're living successfully?: You may say that it's easy to talk about unconditional love in an abstract or theoretical way — but what does it mean in practice? A useful test, I suggest, would be to ask yourself a number of questions, such as the following:

— How much of your energy is expended on worry (e.g., about money, family, work, relationships)?

• *Your rate of success is diminished to the extent that you worry at all. (Understandably, you may feel that it's asking the impossible of any human being not to worry; but it's a habit which you can break — for example, by handing things over to your guides.)*

— How possessive are you (e.g., of spouse, lover, children, material things)?

• *Successful living is always limited by possessiveness.*

— How tolerant are you of all others (e.g., their views, behaviour)?

• *Successful living doesn't allow for any exceptions; that doesn't mean, of course, that you have to agree with everybody.*

— How jealous/envious are you of others (e.g., their possessions, looks, fame, lovers)?

• *Not at all, ideally.*

— Do you hate, resent,or feel angry towards, another/others on a continuing basis?

• *Allow for your humanity — in occasional bursts!*

— How much are you controlled by a need to project a certain image of yourself (e.g., your perception of how you wish another/others to see you)?

• *Again,ideally, not at all.*

— How sincere are you in your relationship with others?

• *Not an easy question; the simplest way to approach it, I suggest, is to use a barometer of how you would wish others to relate to you.*

— How respectful are you of others' space, privacy, free will?

• *A central difficulty with this question is how to distinguish between helpfulness and interference; helpfulness is exploration of potential and choices in non-directive ways and is always geared towards increasing awareness (e.g., how guides/guardian angels operate); interference is controlling and arrogant in its assumption that one knows what's best for another.*

— How comfortable are you with yourself? (e.g., do you impose a burden of perfection —according to your own perception, inevitably — on yourself? Do you regularly observe yourself in a self-critical way? Is it difficult for you to be alone for an extended period? Are you dependent on other people to provide you with entertainment, fulfilment, etc.?)

• *The more you enjoy your own company and/or the company of others without feeling pressure either to be continually with others or continually by yourself, and, of course, the more you accept yourself as you are, the more successful you are.*

— How addictive are you (e.g., to drugs, alcohol, food, sports,sex, television)?

• *Anything that's a controlling factor in your life, in other words, when you feel you can't manage without it, restricts your success; the free spirit enjoys, without being controlled.*

— Do you feel stressed or under pressure in any area (e.g., work, sex, relationship, health)?

• *It's very difficult, if not impossible, to be human and not to feel stressed or under pressure at some times; if the feeling is more constant than random, it's time for remedial action.*

— How open-minded are you in your views and beliefs (as distinct from being tolerant of others)?

• *It's equally important, from a success point of view, that you're as tolerant and open-minded with yourself as you are with others; rigidly-held beliefs (e.g., religious, political, atheistic) are inescapably limiting.*

— How fulfilled do you feel in your creativity?

• *Creation of masterpieces in art, literature, etc., is not a prerequisite for fulfilment. The real criterion, I suggest, is how much you enjoy yourself in how you are and whatever you do. As I have already mentioned, I'll discuss creativity separately later.*

— Do you accept and feel your oneness with God?

• *This is the ultimate question which contains all the others. How you live your life determines how much you are at one with God. An atheist could be more in union with God than an ardent believer (although I don't suppose either of them would be too pleased to hear that!).*

In earlier sessions we have discussed God, creator and creation, in detail. While all souls are uniquely individual, they are each part of God (love). While an atheist may well live his life to a large extent in unconscious unity with God, he consciously separates himself from God. But so, too, does the person who because of his beliefs — usually religious - sees God as a separate entity.

Why conscious acceptance of oneness with God, of God in you, is so important is that then you can align yourself with all the infinite love that is God, thus allowing yourself the opportunities for complete fulfilment in your life.

You don't need to employ any elaborate rituals in order to align yourself more consciously with God. The love that is God is already in you, so all that's needed is to release that love more and more unconditionally to yourself and to all others; I'll be expanding on this later.

Learning from animals

11th January: In earlier sessions we discussed how animals fit into the evolutionary process, how the grand design operates through different stages of growth with consciousness spreading through non-human life until it achieves the capacity to exercise free will in human form.

For the purpose of this session I'm confining our consideration to domestic animals, specifically, dogs and cats, and their relationship with human beings. I have chosen dogs and cats particularly because they are preparing to move more immediately into the human state.

Ideally, dogs and cats live with people and learn from them how to be lovingly human. People, in turn, again ideally, learn from their pets how to make progress on their human journey.

Of course, dogs and cats can't be lumped together, any more than humans can; they have their own characteristics , both as species and individually. I'm only generalising about them for illustrative purposes.

If one accepts that all life is comprehended by the grand design, it goes without saying that it's extremely important that all animals should be treated with respect and love.

When you love a dog or a cat there will be shades of difference in how they respond to you; a cat may, initially at least, seem to be more detached than a dog. But of one thing you can be sure — you will see beyond all doubt how love given freely is returned and multiplied. People can learn from dogs — yes, and cats, too, — how to love unconditionally.

Why is it, then, that, if dogs and cats can love unconditionally so readily, the stages of evolution don't go the other way, in other words, that human beings progress towards becoming dogs and cats? The big difference is, of course, that dogs and cats aren't aware of themselves in the same way as humans are. They act in feeling ways, but the feeling is limited by its lack of awareness of itself; in ultimate expression feelings and thoughts are balanced in loving awareness. When a soul is ready to move from the animal to the human state it has reached a level of consciousness where it will be able to incorporate (!) thinking into its feeling. You'll notice how this works with a child. Initially, a child is very like a dog or a cat in that it responds to life in a totally feeling way; it isn't yet aware of itself as a human being.

A major difficulty for a human as he moves from childhood to adolescence and adulthood is that his conditioning is likely to create an imbalance between his feelings and thoughts; usually, he's controlled by his patterns of thought, which are conditioned by environmental, etc., influences. In observing a dog or a cat, in communicating with it, above all, in loving it, he will be helped to achieve a balance; he will not be able to mask his feelings from a dog or a cat in the same way as he may be with a fellow human. In releasing his feelings for the animal he is helping himself to release them more truly towards people.

Further exploration in the light of evolving consciousness of the boundaries of communication between the spirit and physical worlds

11th–24th January: Many of our previous sessions are littered with references to guides and how you interact with them. (For ease of communication I'm using *you* in a general way.)

As people have moved in their evolution from the instinctual animal to the rational human state they generally seem to think that value accrues with complexity. In spite of unprecedented advances in technology it appears that business can't be conducted without being controlled by all sorts of laws, rules, regulations, involving increasingly diverse specialisms, such as in law, accountancy, taxation. The same thing applies to other areas, such as medicine, religion, legal structures, public institutions; can you think of any exception?

As has been the case in what would tend to be seen as the material world, so, also, complexity has been a feature of people's perception of spiritual echelons, ranging from God to hierarchies of archangels, angels, saints, illuminated Masters, and so on, through multiple levels of perceived holiness or spiritual attainment.

From where I sit (!) there's no complexity, just utter simplicity. Every soul is divine, a part of God. As I outlined (in our first book), some souls — a small minority — lost their awareness of themselves and have been struggling to regain it. Accordingly, there is a transitional period during which there are differing levels of awareness. Ultimately there will be no distinctions; all will be equal, yet uniquely individual, in their regained awareness of their divinity.

In the meantime you are experiencing humanity with all its density while, at the same time, conscious that you're a spirit being temporarily using a physical body. The challenge for you is how to integrate as far as possible the material and spirit worlds.

At present there are many souls in physical and non-physical states (both sides of the border, as it were) involved in finding ways to improve communication between the different states. It is important to bear in mind, though, that this has to be done — or, I should say, needs to be done — with total respect for free will so that souls in spirit do not interfere with the freedom of choice of those who are experiencing physical existence.

In previous sessions we have discussed ways and means of achieving easier communication with guides/guardian angels. (As you know, I make no distinction between guides and guardian angels.) Since you have been patient enough to continue to share our exploration, I'd like to invite you to accompany me in further experimentation and to assure you that it's a great privilege for me that you (dear reader) have agreed to participate, even to this stage, in our voyage towards utopia. You may be interested to learn that in the relatively short time since we embarked on this journey (in 1981) much progress has been made through the efforts of many souls in raising awareness on a global scale.

Let's look at how you communicate with each other in the physical world. You talk, listen (sometimes!), sing, make music, laugh, smile, write, use technology (e.g., telephones, radio, television, computers), advertise, make love, stay silent, make gestures, play games, fight, touch, give presents, paint, sculpt, cook, share material possessions, go into partnerships, reach out to each other in all sorts of ways. By and large, you accept all those forms of communication as a matter of course. Sometimes your communication is fully conscious (e.g., making a telephone call — maybe!), sometimes it isn't (e.g., body language). In any case, it's all part of your daily living.

The main difference between physical and spirit states is that souls in spirit don't have to operate in form or structure; for example, they don't need language, as you know it; communication happens telepathically. (That's just as well, you might say, as you can imagine the confusion there would be if souls in spirit, who are not confined by national boundaries or ethnic groupings, had to contend with language barriers; anyway, all your languages and dialects resulted from limited, because physical, mobility; people in a particular region, who wouldn't have known of the existence of other areas, developed their own peculiar methods of communicating with each other.) That doesn't mean that in spirit souls are deprived of sound. Those who like sound can have all they want of it; those who don't needn't tune into it. It's rather analagous to somebody using ear attachments listening to radio or television having the benefit of sound without intruding on anybody else's silence.

Incidentally, if it weren't possible for souls in spirit to experience sound, you can easily imagine what a profound culture shock it would be for any of your present sound-oriented younger generations who might find themselves catapulted (by "dying") into a soundless non-physical state. Perish the thought!

In earlier sessions I explained in some detail why communication between guides and humans, as built into the grand design, needed to be unobtrusive. Essentially, a balance had to be found between giving help and non-interference with free will. There's no rigidity in the grand design; it adjusts itself continuously to evolving consciousness; this adjustment is reflected in the form of communication considered desirable at any particular time.

The material in these sessions couldn't be given physical clothing without the cooperation of a human agent. The time sequence might give an impression that the material is being doled out on a piecemeal basis; but, actually, it reflects expansion of consciousness in the human receiver, and also seeks to accommodate itself to those who are persevering with us in our adventure. At this stage on our journey, it seems to me that the time is right for us, together, to see how we can go further with breaking down the barriers of communication between the physical and spirit states. I would like to outline certain suggestions and considerations some of which will be reminders of material already given but which I have included for ease of reference and in order to provide a readily-accessible "package".

✳   ✳   ✳

1   It is hardly necessary to say that your acceptance of yourself as a spirit being, a soul who happens to have temporarily taken on physical form, is a basic first step.

2   Acceptance that you have guides who link in with you and whose purpose is to help you fulfil your potential is desirable.

3   Release yourself from conditioning as far as you can; in case this sounds like a tall order, see it in terms of being open-minded and non-judgemental, without being controlled by rigid beliefs or absolutism.

4   The more relaxed you are the easier the flow of communication will be; anxiety, e.g., trying too hard, creates a blockage.

5   Ask your guides to keep your aura free from negative energies; it would be an interference with your free will for your guides to do that without your consent; you need ask only once.

6   Consider how impressions come to you normally.For instance: do you tend to get visual images easily? Do you operate more on a feeling level? Are you comfortable with ideas? Do you understand things better when you write them down? Do you find that you just know things at times without having to go through a logical process to work them out? Your guides will tend to develop communication with you through your particular style.

7   The main difficulty with this sort of communication is how to know whether it's really happening. In your day to day life you meet people, you talk to them, they answer you, you can touch them, if you want to, and you have no doubt about that sort of reality. Similarly, you talk to somebody by telephone, or you hear somebody talking on radio, or see somebody on television, and you accept that that's real. Normally, you can't see or hear a guide in so obvious a way. How then can you know whether you're in direct communication with a guide or not?

8   You may remember that I used an analogy of a jigsaw puzzle to illustrate how all souls are linked together in consciousness (in God) but yet that each soul has its own unique place in the cosmic design. As you grow in awareness you tap into that consciousness more and more which is another way of saying that you integrate increasingly with you as oversoul. That is, of course, your overall purpose in coming into your present physical lifetime, and your guides are constantly helping you to fulfil that purpose. As your awareness increases, you are, to a continually magnifying extent, automatically in tune with your divine consciousness, so that your own feelings and thoughts are on a wavelength with those of your guides and of you yourself as oversoul. That's why you may not feel guidance coming to you in an obvious manner as if from outside of you. You are allowing God to manifest in you, which is reflected in your feelings and thoughts.

9   Suppose you feel you have a decision to make about something. I'm taking it for granted that you have already gone through the steps which I have outlined above. You have asked your guides to help you with the decision, so you let go as far as you can of any preconceived ideas and wait and see what comes to you. This is where the considerations referred to at paragraph 6 above are relevant; an answer is likely to come to you in a way that suits your style. If no clear answer comes to you immediately, don't worry; sometimes the process of decision-making works out better when it's given breathing space.

If your guides can't get through to you directly (e.g., if you're too anxious), they will find other ways of reaching you, for example, through somebody else, or a dream, or by nudging you to read something or listen to, say, a radio programme.

10 The more you integrate with something, the less you notice it as separate. That's why people are often disappointed when they find that what began as very obvious communication with guides is no longer so; some people then start questioning themselves and wondering where they have "gone wrong". They haven't, of course; rather, they have "gone right"!

11 All the same you say, "I'd love to be able to have a chat with a guide occasionally in the same way as I would with a (human) friend. Why couldn't that be fitted into the grand design? Surely now that I've taken all the preparatory steps you've outlined and I understand how guidance works, an occasional chat could only have the effect of helping me to increase my awareness?" You may not have any specific problem or pressure of decision-making at all, but you'd simply like to have a chat. Fair enough.

12 In the utopian state, which I predicted would come into being in 2030 (*the fourth book*), communication between the spirit and physical worlds will be commonplace. Initially this will involve only a tiny proportion of the (physical) world's population. Even now, though, with the phenomemal acceleration in the movement of consciousness which has been taking place in recent years many people are ready to cooperate in a venture (or, maybe more appropriately, an adventure), which will bring about dramatic change in people's perception of life and, indeed, in how they live.

13 I must remind you that what we're attempting now has never before happened on earth. Many souls on this (non-corporeal!) side have been waiting eagerly for enough souls on earth to be ready to go ahead with experimentation in breaking down the barriers between the spirit and physical worlds. I'm not talking

now about the occasional mediumistic communication which has flourished sporadically through the centuries, or about something "paranormal" which has hitherto been confined to a small number of people who have been regarded as particularly psychic or spiritual or more likely, "odd", but, rather about developments which will be open to all those who wish to prepare themselves to avail of them.

14   So, then, you're ready and willing to participate in this experimentation. What do you need to do? How can you bring about a situation where you can have a chat with a guide or with a relative or friend who is now in spirit?

15   I would recommend that you initially confine yourself to experimenting with a guide. Later, as you see how you progress with that, you can, if you wish, ask your guide to facilitate the other type of communication for you. In general, it is desirable, in order to avoid interference with privacy, that communication with a "dead" friend or relative should only be arranged through a guide.

16   At present it is not possible for a guide to appear before you or beside you in a form that you can readily see and touch, so that you won't have the same immediate proof that you have with a physical associate. The situation is unbalanced as far as you are concerned in that the guide is more obviously aware of you than you are of the guide.

17   Given that physical presence is not feasible, communication has to be arranged rather like a telephone conversation minus the sound. (My analogy is with non-visual telephonic communication.) When somebody contacts you by telephone you're aware of the caller before you can hear a voice, and you don't have to pinch yourself and ask "Is it just my imagination playing tricks on me?". Before you lift the telephone you get a signal — the ringing tone — and you know that there's somebody at the other end of the line. Similarly, you can arrange to have a signalling system with a guide or guides which will be your

way of satisfying yourself that you're having authentic communication.

18   Just to be clear — what we're talking about here is the situation at your end. Guides don't need any signals in order to tune into you; as I've already said, they're only a thought away from you.

19   If you want to have a chat with a guide, I suggest that you ask for an agreed signal that you will continue to use as a lead-in to your communication. For example, Sara accepts that she has guides helping her on her human journey. She feels that she would like to establish a more conscious link with at least one of them. She relaxes as much as she can in whatever way best suits her and she sends a thought to her guides expressing her wish and asking for a signal. Because her visual faculties are strong, in other words, she understands something more easily when she can put a visual image on it, her guides will be likely to show her a picture, e.g., of a flower, or a bird, or an animal, or an object that's familiar to her. Whenever, then, she "rings up" a guide and that image flashes on her "screen", she can accept that she's in a two-way communication with a guide.

20   For people who aren't comfortable, or don't feel confident, with visual images, other signals will be used, e.g., a shivery or tingly feeling, a word, an impression of being touched, a feeling of an in-flow of energy or of being gently rocked. The main thing is that it should be an easy signal which would also be unmistakable.

21   While guides are, of course, friends, their aim is to help people regain lost awareness, so that will always be a primary consideration in their communication with you. You will notice that there's always subtlety in the guidance you receive, particularly as you progress in your intercourse. Accordingly, don't expect matters to be set out for you in a black and white way. In the nature of things, you are more likely to wish to have communication with your guides when you want something;

that's understandable because you're still struggling with humanity, while your guides have moved beyond that — lucky devils! (An interesting colloquialism; why should devils, given their place in religious orthodoxy, be considered lucky? is it that they don't have to be "good", and so can have all the fun they like?!) All the same, you might bear in mind that your guides like to hear from you, too, when things are going smoothly for you — just to send greetings, or thanks, or love; they're not looking for gratitude, but it expands your energy when you express it.

Criticism — and how to deal with it

25th January: In this session I'm talking about criticism in its narrow meaning of finding fault, rather than as evaluation of, say, art, drama, literature; in other words, in its negative, rather than positive, clothing.

Criticism is a great leveller. It is probably the biggest barrier of all to self-expression. It is all-pervasive in that it works both from the inside and the outside, the self-critic as well as the self-appointed one.

Criticism that comes from outside is of no importance in the long run, or, at most, it's only important if you allow it to affect you.(Easier said than done!) Whether you are self-critical, or to the extent that you are, is all that matters.

Since people aren't born, and don't live, in isolation from each other, there's bound to be interaction between them. Physical existence, as you know it, is ordered in communities of continents, nation/states, indigenous arrangements, families. Usually, there are laws, customs and cultural mores which create expectations in general and specific ways as to how people should live their lives. Accordingly, it can seem to be a safe way for a person to get by if he doesn't draw attention to himself by being "different" unless the attention results from some achievement, or way of life, which is generally regarded as praiseworthy.

How did you become self-critical? Through a combination of circumstances. As a soul on a continuing journey towards regaining lost awareness, you will more than likely have experienced a number of physical lifetimes, effects from which you carried through into your present life. You chose to be born into an environment which would be likely to help you to deal with those effects, probably by facing you with them through your contact with people around you. For example, your parents are seen as respected members of the community; that's the public image of your family grouping. At home, however, there's a lot of tension, with no real communication between your parents. You, being very sensitive, are affected by the tension, without knowing its source. Perhaps, you think, you are the cause of it. One or both of your parents may be preoccupied and not available to listen to you or take notice of you. Maybe there's something wrong with you that they're like that? What can you do to get their attention, their approval? You begin to watch yourself, to be self-conscious, to analyse people's reactions to you as you perceive them. Your inner critic is becoming well established, nurtured and blooming (a blooming nuisance!). At school, a teacher makes disparaging remarks about your efforts at art or music or writing and your creative expression is stunted; better to play safe and do something useful, functional, with your life; whatever you do, don't leave yourself open to being a target for somebody to downgrade or humiliate you!

You exist, then, on a superficial level without ever giving yourself a chance to explore your deeper, innermost, creativity. You will probably have convinced yourself that you're not at all creative, and so to a large extent you waste the potential which you provided for yourself in undertaking a physical transition.

That's just one scenario. Opportunities to develop and reinforce self-critical faculties are myriad. People in your life, from your parents onwards, are catalysts in one way or another. They all mirror you to yourself in how you relate to them. Your strength is determined by how free from control you are in your interaction with them.

If somebody is behaving in a critical manner towards you, what's happening? That person is seeing you, or aspects of you, from his perspective, his place in the jigsaw. He cannot be aware, no matter how well he thinks he knows you, of what's really going on inside you, your feelings, your thoughts, your inner motivation. The same thing applies, of course, if you are critical of another.

Once you accept in both your feelings and thoughts that nobody is in a position to tell you how to live your life, that, irrespective of whatever authority any person may arrogate to himself in expressing a judgement on you or your behaviour,your life on earth is your journey and only yours, you will be able to listen in a detached way to any criticism. If there are aspects of it that make sense to you, you'll be in a position to assess them objectively and respond to them constructively.

Ultimate security lies in accepting and feeling God in you, and in acknowledging that God is also in everybody else,Then you won't be inclined to find fault with anybody, including, of course, yourself.

How to release your creative potential

25th January–2nd February: In our recent sessions I have repeatedly mentioned creativity, and I promised to discuss it separately. As I have already said, everybody, without exception, is creative, but the trouble is that most human beings either aren't aware of their own creative potential or don't get a chance to express it.

What constitutes creativity? The birth of a baby, certainly. Suppose somebody writes a book that no publisher will accept for publication, or paints a picture that nobody will buy, or composes music that nobody considers worth playing, or designs a building that by general consensus is an eyesore, or so on, is that creativity? Is creativity in so far as literature, art, etc., are concerned to be measured by critical acceptance of them?

In my view, creativity can't be defined by any popular perception of it. It has a multitude of forms — apart from the obvious procreative one - such as, writing a poem, a play, a short story, a book, a letter, painting a picture, a wall, sculpting, designing a bridge, a building, planting a flower, a tree, making love, a cake, a dress,composing a song , a symphony, playing a musical instrument, singing, acting, direction (of plays, movies), photography, filming, storytelling, dancing, sport, computer programming, mechanical inventiveness, embroidery, tapestry, carpentry, flower arranging, hairdressing, farming; in fact, however a person is, or whatever he does, is creative in some form. Each person will perform the most routine procedures in his own style which is peculiar to him alone.

In this session, then, when I'm talking about releasing creative potential what I mean is finding fulfilment.

In our last book we took a look at the emerging future (in your terms; continuing present in mine) of planet Earth. In utopia everybody will be fulfilled. Unfortunately, however, realisation of utopia, while initially attainable for some people in a relatively short period of time, will extend throughout the planet in stages of seemingly tortoise-like progression. (In choosing an image of a tortoise I mean to convey optimism related to the legendary endurance of the tortoise in reaching its goal.)

Most people on the planet, then, will, for many years ahead, have to exist in an interim situation where they needs must conform to restrictive systems and spend much of their waking time performing work which they wouldn't choose to do if they didn't have to provide an income for themselves and their dependants, if any, or in being unable to find remunerative employment at all. How are they going to find fulfilment?

I have gone into this question in some detail earlier (in our last book, too), but I feel that we could usefully explore it more deeply. I'd like to suggest ways by which greater degrees of fulfilment can be achieved, no matter how restrictive you may consider your present situation to be.

✳   ✳   ✳

1   Do you believe that life on earth is intended to be a penitential, self-sacrificing, journey, which, if endured patiently, will lead to eternal reward in heaven? Or do you believe that it's okay to be happy while you're on earth, or, even, that you deserve to be happy? If the former, you're in a mindset which finds fulfilment (if that's the appropriate word!) readily to hand in existing conditions on earth. At this stage my words will have relevance only for those who subscribe to the latter belief — and my hope is, of course, that more and more people will shift from the first category to the second.

2   As your life has evolved you'll have found that you enjoy some
    activities more than others. Make a list of what you enjoy. How
    much do those items feature in your day to day life? Do any of
    them manifest in your present work? If you are unemployed, are
    any of them relevant to your present lifestyle?

3   Apart from what you have found that you enjoy, what dreams
    did you have as a child or as you grew into adulthood of what
    you would like to be or do? Please add those dreams, if any, to
    your list. What stopped you from realising them? What would it
    take to make them a reality? Would you, in fact, want them to
    materialise for you now if you had the means to make that hap-
    pen?

4   As you proceed with your exploration, you will notice how your
    creativity has been continually expressing itself even though
    you were probably not at all aware of it. For example, your taste
    in reading, movies, theatre, sport, hobbies, conversation, friends,
    will be likely to have been subject to wide variation through
    your life so far. Imperceptibly, you are constantly evolving and
    the you that you are expressing today is different in some degree
    from the you of yesterday.

5   Accordingly, in making your lists it's important to bear in mind
    that what you enjoy doing today you may not enjoy tomorrow.
    People may feel frustrated in their present existence because
    they see no opportunity to follow their dreams. But how often
    has it transpired that, for those who at some stage found such
    opportunities, the reality turned out to be totally disappointing?

6   Ideally, what you want is that you will be able to live your life
    in a continuing enjoyment of every moment, accepting that you
    have only the present moment, since you can't live in the past or
    the future, and bearing in mind that sources of enjoyment for
    you may be subject to constant or periodic change. Is there any
    point, then, you may well ask, in making lists, as I have suggest-
    ed, of what you enjoy at present and/or your dreams? The rea-
    son why I have suggested making the lists is that by doing so

you are focusing your energy and looking at how you're living your life; if, for example, you see yourself as being trapped in a continuing round of duties, responsibilities, financial pressures, relationship problems, non-stimulating work, and so on, you are locked into a negative pattern of energy which is self-perpetuating. Understandably, you might say that it's easy for me in my celestial(!) smugness to expound simplistic diagnoses, but *you* are stuck with coping with the physical realities as they are.

7   No matter how much you may seem to be a victim of circumstances you still have the power to change your life. That power is within you; you can exercise it positively or negatively. One thing is certain: there will not be positive direction in your life unless you decide to make it so.

8   Once you make the decision that you want to express yourself in your living in a manner that will provide you with creative fulfilment and at present you feel that you can find such fulfilment in the ways outlined in your lists, I suggest that you then hand over the lists to your guides, thereby aligning yourself with all the evolved energy of the universe (God) and enabling opportunities to manifest in line with your unfolding and perhaps changing perceptions of sources of enjoyment for you. In the handing over process you are accepting that you have set the wheels in motion for you to be supported by the infinite, universal energy (God) through (a) exercising your own free will, (b) giving positive direction to your energy by outlining how you'd like to express yourself, while understanding that you are doing this in accordance with your present perceptions of what you want and allowing yourself flexibility to respond to your changing perceptions in the knowledge and trust that your guides are keeping a constant overview of your (soul) purpose; and (c) acknowledging that you need help.

9   When the time comes for you to say thanks to your body and leave it, and you look back on your physical journey, your review of it won't be concerned with how much possessions you acquired, what recognition you achieved, what status you

earned, etc.; your only concern, ultimately, will be to what extent you were able to release and enjoy your creative potential, in other words, your divinity. My earnest wish is that the questions I have raised and the suggestions I have made will help you towards that end.

Dialogue with Shebaka

8th February–16th March: **Patrick Francis** I accept and, indeed, I know that there are at present all sorts of global evidences of growth in awareness in a general way. But at the same time there seems to be a lot of unrestrained violence; for example, some people appear to have no qualms about torturing and killing helpless elderly men and women; not to mention, of course, the mass horrors that are all too often perpetrated in different parts of the world. Do you still feel optimistic about the planet?

Shebaka Yes. Violence in all its forms is an expression of inner conflict. When all people find peace in themselves there will be no violence. I'm optimistic because I can see how many people are looking, and are beginning to look, within themselves. All through the evolution of the planet, people have been looking to gods and gurus of one kind or another to tell them what to do. Now more and more people are accepting that the divine is within each of them and as they let it manifest they love themselves and each other unconditionally. Of course, it's a gradual process, and the conflict in change can be intense. Freedom, once surrendered, is not easily regained. But the tide of divine love, as people are now allowing it to express itself in them, is flowing too strongly to be turned back.

PF I know that in the utopian scheme of things there won't be any crime and, therefore, no need for penal systems. In the meantime society is burdened with hugely expensive systems of law enforcement, often culminating in locking people up for varying periods of time with little or no rehabilitative effects — in fact, the reverse in many cases. Have you any comments or suggestions?

S I'm sure there would be general agreement — certainly amongst our readers — that the ideal situation would be one where all people would be at peace with one another with total respect for each individual's "space". Obviously, that would mean that there would be no violation of anybody's person or territory. It would follow that there would be no need for the present panoplies of law enforcement arrangements.

Even looked at purely from an economic point of view that sounds eminently sensible, doesn't it? And if it is true that the vast majority of people would want it why isn't it happening?

The simple answer is that most people are not yet at peace within themselves — although, as I have said earlier, I'm optimistic about the rate of progress in that direction — and this is reflected outwardly in conditions around them. That's why I have been concentrating so much in our sessions on the need for each individual to look within first and to find the liberation of taking responsibility for himself. Any community is a reflection of the individuals who comprise it. The more each individual finds fulfilment, the more the community will benefit. That's obvious, isn't it?

A central question, then, is — how can things be orchestrated in such a way that all people individually will have opportunities to expand their awareness and release their divinity within their humanness? That would mean putting interim arrangements in place as a prelude to the utopian situation.

In general, people who are sentenced to terms of imprisonment feel themselves marginalised in one way or another by the society in which they live. It's true that they will have chosen to be born into that society for their own individual reasons. So, ought we take the view that, since that's their choice, it would be an interference with their purpose to attempt to ameliorate their present condition? If we follow that line we're taking a very rigid stance — applying a literal interpretation to the maxim *as you sow so shall you reap* — which would mean that no helping hand could ever be given to anybody;

for instance, there would be no point at all in having guides/ guardian angels.

Everybody on earth is ultimately aiming to get off the roundabout of cause and effect; clearly that's still an unconscious aim for most of the planet's population. If the systems under which people exist can be changed in order to provide more opportunities for them to find creative fulfilment, that's automatically going to help raise awareness. So now, if you agree, we'll take a look at how the systems can be changed.

We're starting from the base that there would be no crime if all people were at peace within themselves. In our last session we considered in some detail how people can release their creative potential, which, of course, would have the effect of helping them to achieve inner peace. Our challenge,then, is to suggest ways and means by which existing administrative arrangements can facilitate the release of creative potential within everybody without exception.

The scale of the challenge is obvious when we take into consideration the diversity of human existence. Not alone are there all the differing age levels but also the vast gaps in social and material circumstances as well as individual inclinations and capabilities.

I don't want to denigrate the various social and political reforms that have been implemented throughout human history. That they have — to date — been unsuccessful can hardly be denied, but they have been part of an evolutionary process which has brought people to a greater awareness than ever before of how what affects one affects all.

Where do we start? Where else but at the beginning of human life — with children?

It goes without saying that it's vitally important that children should be loved and encouraged to express themselves freely. Educational systems should be organised, I suggest, in ways which would facilitate exploration and expression of each child's creative abilities. This would necessarily mean that there would be no set curricula, or, put another way, that there would be an unlimited range of curricula. Each child would get individual attention to a much greater extent than is possible at present. Much increased resources would need to be concentrated in education — in its expanded meaning of drawing forth — but the additional expenditure involved would be more than offset by the resultant elimination of the need for negative punitive measures.

As you know, the reason why the grand design provided that people would be born as children was so that they would be able to make fresh starts. Every child is vulnerable and lovable, and deserves to be loved. No matter what their past life influences may be, children are not born as criminals. Those of them who later get involved in what are regarded as criminal activities do so as a result of environmental influences and their own reaction to them.

Your question referred particularly to prisons. In my view, prisons are as sores or boils on the face of humanity; they are a negative rather than a positive concentration of energies.

PF A big difficulty is that there are such high levels of unemployment.

S The energies of the planet are being used unproductively in many ways. There are more than adequate resources available to provide fulfilling employment for all those who wish to be employed if those resources were to be used in positive rather than negative ways. For example, the purpose of prisons is to lock up people who have been tried and found guilty of having seriously transgressed against a society's laws. Both the prisoners themselves and the custodial staff are bound together in an enclosed cocoon of energy which is damaging for all of them. If it were so that all prisoners, or even a majority of them, find a prison term helpful in increasing their spiritual awareness, prisons might be said to serve a useful purpose. Unfortunately, the opposite is more often the case — a prison term offers opportunities for advanced training in the practical application of criminology!

PF Other options are tried, such as open style institutions for those convicted of what are regarded as less serious offences, or applying probationary and/or community service formulas under supervision, but society, in its majority opinion, demands for its protection that those who are found guilty of crimes classified as serious should be locked away so that they are at least out of circulation for some time.

S Complexities always arise from trying to deal with symptoms rather than causes. That's true in all areas of life — look, for example, at the medical field. Governments, or those charged with administering a nation/state's affairs, are then always responding to given situations in ways which are designed to bring immediately expedient results and are continually dealing with one crisis after another. Things don't have to be sorted out all at once. There are many brave pioneering spirits in human form who have already done, and are continuing to do, important work in reforming your educational, etc., systems, and their efforts are drawing attention to the benefits which flow from tackling causes rather than trying to cope with symptom after symptom and getting nowhere.

PF A conveyor belt type organisation seemed to be an efficient and logical use of resources in that a person needed to have expertise in one area only. I understand that the impetus for that sort of development came by way of assembly line production of cars. Now, of course, specialisation figures largely in all sorts of areas — medicine, law, etc. The rational side of us as human beings likes to break everything into its component parts, so it is an understandable perception that each part could be most effectively dealt with by specialists. Somewhere along the line, though, I think that the human — or, I suppose, really the soul — factor has been missed out. Even though we may often allow ourselves to be treated like robots, deep down we don't like it — I feel — I hope!

S Each soul, whether on its human journey or in spirit, will always have its own particular areas of interest, so that there will eternally tend to be specialisation of some kind. Ultimately, for the soul who has regained full awareness it's rather like specialisation within generalisation — in other words, each soul has immediate access to whatever there is(because it has the ability to link in at all times with the totality of consciousness), but chooses to express itself according to its present inclination. That awareness and freedom are not yet available to those experiencing humanity.

PF Given the compartmentalisation that obtains here on earth at present are we stuck with, for instance, our prison systems as they are?

S It would be unhelpful and impractical for me to suggest something as radical as the closing down of all prisons immediately — although that's what I would do. People would probably be inclined to regard me as being too much under the influence of spirit(s) to be taken seriously! Physical reality evolves in stages. The foundation has to be the nurturing of children — all children. Everything will flow from that.

PF What would you do with, say, a man who abducts a woman, rapes and cold-bloodedly kills her? I'm assuming that there's no doubt but that he's the perpetrator. Our ways of dealing with him would be preventative and punitive — to stop him from committing a further such offence and to punish him, either by executing him or locking him up.

S That way has also followed through into the perception of how the "sinner" is dealt with after he dies — punishment for all eternity. The human system mirrors a perception of the spirit one — a perception rather than the reality of how it is.

The victim in this case is the woman. Her time on earth has been arbitrarily cut short, and that can't be changed. No action taken by the state or by anybody else against the man who killed her can restore that particular physical lifetime. So whatever action is taken by the state, apart from its punitive connotations, can only be expressed to be for the common good as a protection for potential other victims and as a deterrent against any further such acts by the man himself or by others. Whether the man is executed or imprisoned does not affect the karmic debt he owes to the woman he abused and killed. Sooner or later he will have to discharge that debt and no institution or no other person can do that for him.

The notion of punishment to fit the crime doesn't help at all in spiritual terms. Spiritually there is only self-punishment; indeed, use of the word 'punishment' at all is misleading because what happens is a process of self-exploration leading to growth in awareness, which may involve making retribution in some form in respect of, say, acts of violence or cruelty. For example, the man whom we're discussing will, inevitably, given his divine nature, at some future time face what he has done and make compensation to the victim of his violence, not necessarily by an exact reversal of circumstances (which wouldn't be doing her any favours) but by helping her in some appropriate way in her self-realisation. The spiritual way is always simple — one is ineluctably faced with oneself and the mirror of one's expression offers no escape from the consequences of that expression; yet, mercifully, there is infinite flexibility in how one can deal with the consequences.

What we're trying to do in our explorations is to reflect as far as possible the way of spirit into the physical world; the culmination of that projection would be the utopian existence which I have already outlined. So, to answer your question I need to explore how far the spiritual way can be applied to your existing physical circumstances.

Spiritually there's never any question of compulsion. No matter how long it takes, each soul, because its free will is sacrosanct, designs its own journey back to awareness — with, of course, as much help as it is willing to receive. So, if the man who is the subject of your hypothetical question is arrested, convicted and sentenced to imprisonment for a number of years, he is not a willing participant in those procedures and is being compelled to comply with them by the state rather than by his own choice. The state assumes the role which much of your religious tradition ascribes to God in eternal terms — although the state is more merciful in that the time scale of the punishment is usually limited!

PF If we leave compulsion out of the reckoning, what's left? Does that mean that the man continues on his merry way, free, maybe, to commit similar acts of violence against others? And, if so, wouldn't others be encouraged to follow his example without any fear of repercussions?

S As I have already said, the man will, sooner or later, be his own judge, as will all others be their own judges, including those who may allow themselves to be influenced by his example. But, of course, I understand that your question applies to the limited context of the physical framework and, taken on that basis, that there must be some response to the man's actions by the state which is representing not alone his immediate victim but all other potential victims.

PF But how can the state make an effective response — or, indeed, any response at all — without compulsion being involved?

S If the state's response is to put the man in prison and/or execute him, it is committing an act of violence against him, however justifiable that act may seem to be in the light of "the common good". Therefore, prisons or capital punishment cannot be an ingredient in my answer. At the same time, the man's action cannot be ignored. I suggest that the ideal (spiritual) response would be to publish widely details of what happened as well as a profile of the man himself. That would not be an interference with his free will but would focus attention on him in a way that would encourage him to take responsibility for his actions — rather than the state attempting to do so, which is what happens at present.

PF What's to stop him changing from place to place and finding anonymity in that way?

S Nothing — but your state systems provide the means to identify him wherever he goes.

PF But that would mean that he could be ostracised all his life, which would be a more severe punishment than being confined in prison for a certain number of years.

S It wouldn't be intended as punishment at all but rather as a discharge of the function of government — as the agency democratically established by the people to administer the affairs of the state

— to keep the people informed of whatever might be likely to affect them (positively or negatively). How people would respond to the man would be up to each individual, and would potentially be as varied as that. The man might perceive it as punishment, of course — but that would be his choice.

You see, if I may use the parallel of the spirit state, the (non-physical) soul is in a vibration where everything is revealed. Suppose, for example, everybody in the physical world was able to see, immediately and completely, everybody else's aura. Then nothing would be hidden — the aura would reveal information about people individually which they would often wish to conceal. So, in order to even things up, as it were, and to apply spiritual considerations to the physical state, the nearest answer, in my view, is to reveal information along the lines we have discussed where somebody has obviously and forcefully invaded another's privacy.

PF I took an extreme example of somebody who commits rape and murder. There are the muggers, the burglars, the so-called petty criminals. And there are those who perpetrate acts of mass violence, such as planting bombs, supposedly for political ends. How can they be allowed to ride roughshod over the wishes, privacy and physical safety of others? They feel marginalised already; won't they feel even more so if they're branded publicly and identifiably as criminals?

S Okay, you're on your own , sitting at home, reading a book or looking at television — just doing whatever you feel like doing and enjoying your own company. Your doorbell rings. You answer it. Two men knock you down and kick you senseless. When you recover consciousness and are able to move, albeit painfully, around the house, you find that many of your valued possessions are gone.

Those men abused you, violated your "space" and stole your property. You may well have to endure long term effects from your injuries. Understandably, you are likely to be feeling angry, shocked, afraid, distressed — any number of mixed emotions.

Whatever develops, the physical damage that has been inflicted on you will not be undone. Your injuries will probably eventually heal; if the contents of your home were insured you may be able to replace some or all of the stolen property, and with the passage of time you may be able to relax and enjoy the comfort of your home again.

As soon as you can you report the burglary to your local police. As a result of their investigations they establish the identities of the burglars.

It may give you some emotional satisfaction if the two men are put in prison, but clearly that's not going to be of any real benefit to you. You may say that it will stop them — temporarily — from doing the same thing to another or others, which will please you. However, from a spiritual point of view, the difficulty is that, by depriving the men of their liberty, the state, on your behalf and on behalf of the common good, is invading the men's space, as they invaded yours.

The spiritual principle never changes. Free will is always sacrosanct and not subject to interference or control. I acknowledge that adherence to that principle seems very difficult, if not impossible, in your physical circumstances.

My answer in this case is still the same — publish the details with the identities and descriptions of the burglars.

PF Isn't that invading their privacy?

S They created a public profile for themselves by their action; in other words, they surrendered their own privacy. It is up to themselves whether they want to maintain a public profile or not.

PF How effective would publicity — of a personal kind — be against bombers — on the assumption that their identities could be established?

S I might turn the question back to you and ask you — how effective is imprisonment? I think you will agree that, historically, the answer is not at all. Draconian measures ultimately always fail.

Sometimes they may seem to have a deterrent effect in the short term, but that's all. Invariably they are counterproductive in that they have an inverse inspirational effect. Concentration on negativity reinforces it; so you have an endless cycle of violence seeking to counteract violence.

I understand that what you're doing is playing "devil's advocate" and postulating obvious examples where innocent victims of violence may be left without physical protection. What's basically needed is to create a climate where all people can co-exist in peace. That cannot be done as long as punitive practices are in operation. Whether they are state or individually administered is irrelevant.

PF I think I'm safe in concluding that you're not in favour of imprisonment — not to mention capital punishment!

S You'll hardly be punished for jumping to conclusions!

PF I'm still concerned, though, about your suggested solution — even though I accept that it's an interim one until more radical systems of education are implemented. I'm leaving aside for the moment doubts about the potential effectiveness or otherwise of your solution and wondering about the isolationism that seems to be inherent in it. For example, if I commit a burglary and the details are publicised, including my identity, isn't that like putting a stamp or brand on me that I'll be burdened with wherever I go? Wouldn't that be likely to create in me a grudge against society? Once I'm branded mightn't I as well continue to burgle? Even if I'm very sorry and decide that I never want to do anything like that again, how will I ever free myself from the brand?

S Your act of committing a burglary creates the isolation. In doing it you will have separated yourself from your own divinity, which is *the* isolation. If I, as a spirit (non-physical) being, attempt to intrude on others without their consent, or to control them in any way, I automatically exclude myself from an intimacy of communication with them; in other words, I will have separated myself in consciousness from them; if you like, I will have branded myself. Then I will have put myself into a position of having to regain the awareness I had lost. I can only do that myself — although I can avail myself of all the help I'm willing to receive.

In my situation the consequences of my action would be immediately apparent — like a blot on my aura, if I may use an analogy which would make sense to you. However, where you are concerned, because of the density of the physical vibration, the effect on your aura would not be obvious. That's why, if we are endeavouring to synthesise the spirit and physical vibrations, people need to be alerted to the fact that you are a potential intruder on their space.

An immediate and effective way for you to free yourself from the brand would be to make restitution in some form to those whom you have robbed. That action would then also be publicised. If you're not willing to make restitution (which needn't necessarily be of a financial nature) you're not ready to let the brand go.

PF If I commit murder, though, I can't make restitution — I can't restore physical life to the victim.

S You could convey your sorrow to the victim through your guides, or even just through your thoughts, and you could offer to perform some appropriate service(s) for the victim's family. How acceptable all that would be to the victim or the victim's family would be a matter for them; in any event, your offer would be a public apology.

PF Under our present systems crimes are investigated by police and courts with the aim of establishing guilt or innocence without doubt. How would you compensate for that?

S As I have said, ideally there's always a gradualism about change on earth. The first priority is education. That will automatically lessen the incidence of crime. I would next begin to phase out the penal institutions. This would be an inevitable progression once the focus of communities would be lovingly rather than fearfully oriented.

PF But suppose somebody is falsely accused and found guilty. A serious injustice would be done to him by his being publicly stigmatised as a criminal.

S Yes, but at least he would be more free to get on with his life — and perhaps to prove his innocence — than if he were shut away in prison.

I would wish that circumstances would never arise where it would be necessary to draw attention to anybody in a way such as I have postulated. That's an unrealistic hope at this stage, unfortunately.

PF I can see — or I think I can — how what you're suggesting would work in spirit where you're not concerned with material issues, such as money, property, and you don't have to cope with the effects of physical injuries, but here on earth where people are looking for visible forms of preventative measures, such as police, courts, prisons — your ideas would be likely to be dismissed by many people as being quixotic.

S I know. But ask yourself — has experience shown that burglaries, rapes, murders, etc., have been eliminated or even lessened because of perceived deterrent effects of all your law enforcement agencies? All the calls for more laws, more police, more prison places, are reinforcing a climate of fear which feeds violence in one form or another. Radical change is needed, with the central spotlight on education and the fulfilment of creative potential. Fortunately — and designedly — there are many people now on earth who are attuned to that consciousness. That's why I'm optimistic.

Adventure in spirit

18th March–20th April: Through the ages people have sought ways and means of transcending the limitations of the physical world. For example, some have concentrated their inventiveness in technological directions with remarkable results; others have developed their physical skills through, for instance, sporting achievement; still others have managed the seemingly extraordinary feat of appearing to be in two places at the same time (bi-location).

In your physical manifestation it's very difficult for you to accept or, indeed, understand that instant creation is a fact of life. In spirit terms there's no problem with that idea — at least as soon as a soul becomes accustomed to being "dead" — because it's immediately obvious; as I have explained earlier, if a soul thinks of, or imagines, something, it manifests instantaneously (like rubbing a magic lantern!). On the other hand, if you in your human state think of something, you usually have no immediate physical evidence of what's created by your thought. Yet creation follows from your thoughts in your human form as surely as it will when you leave the physical state.

What I propose to do in this session is to take you, with your agreement, while you are fully conscious and grounded, on an adventure which is designed to help you transcend the limitations of your present physical dimension and sample how the world of spirit works. You will not be going into trance or an out of body state; at all times you will be in full control and free to continue or discontinue the adventure as you wish.

Please bear in mind that in spirit you are beyond the boundaries of time and space, that there is no confinement and that anything is possible. All that's needed is that you're willing to participate in our adventure and to allow it to happen in whatever way it will. You don't have to worry about whether you have a hangup about visualisations, or whether you're inclined to fall asleep when you try anything like this; just take it as it comes and I promise you that it will work for you at some level.

As always, in order to be more truly yourself the more relaxed you are the better. The biggest barriers to relaxation are invariably thoughts, whether focused on a particular problem or situation or just chasing each other at random. It doesn't matter what form of relaxation you use as long as it suits you and it works. My suggestion, which you may find helpful, would be to sit comfortably, close your eyes and breathe deeply in and out for a few minutes; don't fight or resist whatever thoughts come into your head (resistance always reinforces) and you'll find that they'll fade away, leaving you in a state of peaceful being.

Since what I am conveying to you needs to be embodied in words, and since you can't (yet!) read with your eyes closed, in order to participate in the trip you'll need to pre-record what follows or to arrange to have somebody read it for you.

You have been notified that you have been given a gift of a trip to a location which is being kept secret from you, that all arrangements have been made to have your family, work, etc., looked after while you're away, that you have no need to worry about details of currency, clothes, travel, accommodation — everything is organised so that you haven't a care in the world; all you need to do is to be ready to go at a particular time.

You are willing to accept the gift and at the appointed time you see a magnificent looking limousine stopping outside your home. A man emerges from the car and comes to your front door. When you open the door he informs you that his name is Luke and that he has come to take you on the preliminary part of your adventure. He holds one of the rear doors of the car open for you and you recline into the plush seat. Luke starts the car and it glides smoothly along the road.

In front of you is a cabinet with a variety of drinks and some glasses. A card located prominently on the cabinet reads — Please Help Yourself. You decide that you may as well sample what's on offer and you do. You notice that there's a television set in the cabinet and you switch it on if you feel inclined to do so. Luke thoughtfully leaves you to your own devices without interruption.

Time passes unobtrusively and comfortably. You have made up your mind not to wonder about where you're going but just to enjoy the experience moment by moment. You are completely relaxed. Maybe you even let yourself savour the theatricality of waving royally to imaginary masses of cheering people as you elegantly pass by.

Hardly any time at all seems to have elapsed until you find that you have arrived at an airport runway. Luke stops the car, gets out and opens one of the rear doors, indicating to you that you're going to be travelling on an aeroplane sitting on the runway near the car.

A smiling young woman; greets you and introduces herself as Angela. There's a red carpet leading from the plane to the door of the car. You are hesitant to believe that it was laid on specially for you, but yet that seems to be the case.

Ushered by Angela, you walk along the carpet and up into the plane. You see that there's no other passenger — yet at least — except yourself. The only crew members on the plane seem to be Angela and the captain, who introduces himself as Michael, welcomes you on board and wishes you a pleasant trip. Angela informs you that you are, in fact, the only passenger so that you're free to choose whichever seat you prefer.

You are somewhat flabbergasted to learn that the whole plane is for you only and fleetingly you wonder has there been some mistake, that maybe all the special treatment is intended for some very important public person. As if she's reading your mind, Angela reassures you that there's no mistake, that, yes, the special treatment is for a very important person, and that you are that person. You joyfully experiment with the seats until you find what you like best.

Angela brings you a menu and asks you to choose what you'd like to eat and she also offers you your choice of drinks. There's a luxury of choice from your favourite food and drinks. You make your selections and sit back, wallowing in the enjoyment of what's happening to you.

Easily and smoothly the plane takes off and you rejoice in the feeling of being airborne. Quickly the ground underneath recedes and all below looks smaller and smaller. Soon you're above the white cushion of clouds feeling that you're in a magical cocoon of blissful serenity.

Angela brings you a meal such as would make even the most fastidious gourmet's mouth water; a veritable feast designed to suit your palate. In the unaccustomed feeling of having no pressures of time you experience the meal and, then, replete and relaxed, you allow yourself to enjoy the freedom from day to day responsibilities and duties.

After some time Angela comes to you and tells you that you're about to embark on another phase of your journey. You notice that the plane is coming to a stop, but it's not like the usual way of touching down on a runway — there's no sensation of descending or of contact with the ground.

Angela takes your hand and assures you that there's nothing to fear as she leads you towards the exit.

You step out onto what seems to be a ladder, but again you have no sensation of physical contact. As you reach the foot of the ladder you are surprised to find that you're apparently walking on solid ground but yet seemingly gliding over it.

Reassuringly, Angela stays with you and appears to be completely familiar with the conditions which you are now experiencing. For you, too, there's a familiarity about everything, but yet you feel different. You're not confined in your movements, there's a lightness about you; it's as if you're flying rather than walking; and you have a panoramic view of everything. It's all very beautiful and peaceful.

You ask Angela where are you. She smiles and answers enigmatically that you're not anywhere but that you're at home. You realise that that's all the information you're going to get from her, for the present at any rate, and you allow yourself to continue to be guided by her.

You have arrived at the entrance to a magnificent looking building. Angela leads you through a long hallway. As you go through the hallway you meet people, all of whom greet you familiarly. You notice that nobody seems to have to open doors — they all glide through them. You wonder idly why do they bother with doors at all; probably for appearance's sake, you think.

Soon the same thing happens to you and Angela — you reach a door and you both glide through it. You're in what seems like a vast library. Angela guides you to a particular section of the room and indicates to you to sit in an armchair. She makes a gesture and suddenly you're looking at a movie. The opening credits show you as the star, the producer and the director. As the movie unfolds you see yourself in different roles but you have no doubt that it's you in varying manifestations.

You stay with the movie, allowing it to unfold, knowing that there's no hurry. You may wish to "freeze" some parts of it to give yourself time to absorb a particular scene or scenes.

As the movie draws to a close you see yourself as you now are, and what you set out to accomplish in your life.

When you're ready, the picture fades and Angela takes your hand and leads you from the room.

As you're wondering — what next? — Angela guides you through another door into a room which is occupied by three radiant looking beings. They smile at you and one of them invites you to sit with them, addressing you by name and saying 'welcome back' to you. That doesn't sound odd to you as you feel at home in the room and in that company. Angela, of course, is also sitting with you.

It doesn't seem necessary to use language. It's as if you know automatically what you're communicating to each other. You sense immediately that they are happy to discuss with you the movie you have just seen. If you wish, ask for an evaluation of your progress to date.

If you have any special concerns about yourself and/or others, or if you have unfulfilled dreams, or if you just want to have a general chat about spiritual or material matters, this is a good opportunity for you to look for guidance.

When you feel that you've had enough discussion you all sit silently in loving harmony savouring the unity and the joy of being.

After what may be a little while or a long while you gather from Angela that she will take you on the next part of your trip if you are ready to move. You realise that it's open to you to come and go as you wish. As you take your leave of them you understand from the other three occupants of the room that you will be in constant contact with each other according as you desire it.

Now Angela takes you through a long corridor into another room. She suggests to you that you lie on a bed in the centre of the room. As you do, the bed moulds itself into your shape and is wonderfully comfortable. You find the atmosphere in the room totally relaxing, with muted colour combinations and soft background music.

You are suddenly aware that there are four angelic beings around you, one at your feet, one at your head and one on each side of you. You understand from them that they are there to give you healing, if you so wish. You gladly accept.

Immediately you begin to feel a flow of energy through all parts of your body from the top of your head down to your toes.

As you radiate in the glow of the healing, impressions of the movie which you saw earlier may pass before you. In any case, whether they do or not, the healing which you are now receiving is ranging over your whole evolution since you separated yourself from your full awareness of yourself and of your place in God. You feel all the burdens, the suffering, the guilt, the weariness, the isolation, the sorrow, of humanity lifted from you. You feel your love flowing from you towards yourself, towards all those you hold dear to you and towards all souls; and you forgive yourself for all that followed from your act of separation from your own divinity. All the doubts fade away, there are no more questions to be asked, there's just the ineffable joy of being.

You feel a tap on your shoulder and you see Angela standing smiling beside you. You're no longer aware of the angelic beings. You send thoughts of profound gratitude to them and you rise and go with Angela.

Once again you pass through corridors, smilingly saluting those whom you meet.

You leave the building and soon you find yourself back at the entrance to the plane. Michael welcomes you aboard again and without delay you're settled into your seat and the plane is smoothly on its way. You are still savouring all that you have experienced on your trip when the plane touches down. This time you can feel the contact with the ground and you know you're back on earth.

You thank Angela and Michael, and both of them hug you lovingly as you realise that Luke is waiting for you beside the plane with the same limousine. You sit in the back seat and wave goodbye to Angela and Michael as the car moves easily away.

The homeward bound journey is more internalised and reflective than the outward one. Soon you're safely back outside your front door. You thank Luke and you enter your home basking in the glow of your experience and realising that the gift which you received is intended as a continuing one which is open to you to repeat whenever you wish to do so.

Freedom from negative karmic effects

7th–29th May: I'm using the word 'karma' in the sense of effects accumulated during a soul's progress through its evolution since it fell from grace or got temporarily lost, in other words. On that basis karma has both positive and negative connotations, although in general usage it seems to have been assigned a negative complexion — thrown into a "sin bin", as it were!

In much of your religious tradition there has been a strong emphasis on sin. God, as the Creator, the Supreme Being, was (and still is) perceived as having laid down the standards by which people should live. Deviations from those standards were — and continue to be — seen as transgressions against God's laws and, therefore, attracting eternal punishment unless forgiven by God through repentance on the part of the sinner. As has been the way with most human institutions — particularly the religious ones — fear became a most useful controlling instrument for encouraging obedience to "divine law". Thus, emphasis came to be focused on people's perceived faults rather than virtues.

It's helpful, I think, to observe briefly the development into Christianity of confession and penance. There was a neat simplification in it — a system whereby a person decided, according to a prescribed formula, the ways in which he had offended against God's laws, confessed them to a priest, said he was sorry, and the priest, as God's chosen representative, gave him absolution, subject, perhaps, to his performing a specified penitential ritual; the way was then clear for him to go to heaven unless he subsequently committed more sins — which, of course, he could later confess, provided he wasn't unfortunate enough to die without having made a "good confession."

The emphasis on being good or perfect within a rigid formula of expected behaviour inevitably conditioned people to patterns of self criticism and accrued emotions of unworthiness.

As human evolution moved into the present century, and particularly into the later part of it, confession — which, in any case, had become generally associated with one religious tradition — retained for some its supernatural connotation but on a wider front began to be replaced by psychiatry, psychology, psychotherapy, and other forms of counselling. There's a big difference, of course, in that counsellors do not see themselves as instruments of God's forgiveness, nor do they represent themselves as facilitators of a supernatural or sacramental ritual. However, there's a marked similarity in that both confession and counselling rely on analytical procedures — more deeply so in the case of counselling.

In comparing to some extent confession and counselling I don't want to convey an impression that I'm devaluing either of them. Both have been potentially purveyors of hope without which humanity could have been a cavernous experience. Counselling, in particular, has helped, and continues to help, many people to see themselves in a new light and to deal with heavy burdens of grief, guilt, etc.

My purpose in this session is not to denigrate in any way the efforts of so many wonderful people in helping to raise consciousness but to highlight the fact that in spiritual terms it is now possible to see how a complete shift in consciousness may be achievable. Since people were conditioned to a "sin" culture it was understandable that, even where there was no longer overtly any religious context, counselling practices would focus on what was "wrong" or negative rather than on what was "right" or positive. The trend, then, evolved into discovering and dissecting experiences from a person's childhood onwards which were regarded as "blockages" or generally negative influences. It is important to stress that the admirable overall objective was to eliminate negative effects so that then the person concerned could go on to live in a positive frame of mind.

Here I need to highlight two considerations in particular.

Because a soul in its continuing evolution towards regaining lost awareness takes on many forms and has accumulated a vast range of experiences with consequential effects carried through into successive lifetimes, it is ultimately a futile exercise to attempt to reach a comprehensive explanation and understanding of emotional pressures by attributing them to experiences in the present lifetime; they may be reinforced by those experiences, but that's a deliberate feature of the grand design adapted to the person's own choice. Such an exercise is like walking on shifting sand — there's no firm foothold. (You may well comment that it's strange that the grand design doesn't provide that you can easily remember all the details of your past lives. We have touched on this previously; the simple answer is that the burden would be too much for you to carry — you wouldn't be able to function; as you know, it's often a great mercy to forget details of your present life.)

Focusing on negativity, albeit with a positive aim, locks people into patterns of consciousness which affect how they relate to the world around them — which, in turn, influences what manifests for them in their day to day experiences. The ideal way to live, of course, is totally in the moment, free of the past and the future. As you know, spiritually there's no past or no future — there's only a continuing present, which is how it is perhaps easier to understand that there's no beginning or no end.

That's why in our earliest sessions I talked about the need to eliminate the subconscious which at that time may have seemed a somewhat surprising idea in that the subconscious is often described as a source of inspiration. It isn't; inspiration comes from tapping into the consciousness of the higher self/oversoul, linked to the infinite divine consciousness, channelled, if desired, by guides/guardian angels. The subconscious is the source of fear because it houses emotions indiscriminately. The more you try to live in the past or the future the more you encourage and reinforce the subconscious and, consequently, the more you are controlled by fear. It follows that the more you are involved in a continuing pattern of analysing the past the more you are creating conditions for you to exist fearfully, and, therefore, in your terms, controlling your future because, of course, your today is also your tomorrow as well as your yesterday; the vibrations you send out are constantly creating what transpires for you.

Life, whether in spirit or on earth — the same thing, essentially — is continually evolving and each development, new in its "time", is a stepping stone to another, and so on, which is how stagnation is spiritually restricting. Thus, confession served its purpose at a particular stage in consciousness as also did counselling in its purely analytical form. Now, in my view, the surge of life — a reclaiming of divinity — is demanding something more.

I'd like to interject an analogy of a stream into which a big rock or boulder falls. The rock interrupts the flow of the water and slows it down but it doesn't stop it. When the water gets past the rock — notably, without needing to confront it or remove it — it gathers strength increasingly and ignores obstacles in its way, rather than having to stop to negotiate them, as it is drawn unerringly to the sea, and is then part of the vast energy of the sea. The little stream is in the mighty sea and the sea is in the stream. The stream continues to flow in its own individual way; when it unites itself with the sea it expresses all its power. Always, in whatever measure, it is water, as the sea is.

What's the something more that's demanded? It's the simplicity of the sea being in the stream as the stream is in the sea. Once you accept that through your evolution since you lost your awareness of your divinity you've had countless experiences, thousands of them traumatic and painful ones, you will realise the futility of trying to relive them even in a protected way. In any event, your perception of them as you look back at them would inevitably be different from the way it was as they happened. It isn't possible to re-experience emotions as you will have found out whenever you have attempted to repeat pleasurable sensations; there may be similarities but each experience is new.

My message in this session is that the accumulation of negative karmic effects cannot be released through an intellectual or analytical process by itself. You cannot avoid thinking — not that you'd want to. The ideal situation occurs when feelings and thoughts are balanced so that they become a unity. What usually happens because of the ways your cultures have evolved is that thoughts control feelings. Please bear with me to the extent that I'm repeating myself, but it is essential to keep in mind that your awareness is always expressing itself through your feelings and thoughts and that that's how you're living and will continue to live eternally; that's what you are.

As you exist in the present moment — and can only do so — the conglomeration of experiences which you have had in all your journeying *are of no relevance or importance whatever* except in so far as they continue to control your feelings and thoughts — in other words, how you carry the effects of them in yourself. That means that it's of no value to you to try to assess an experience from an objective or standardised viewpoint — for example, whether it was "good" or "bad" in line with a regulated belief system. Examining an experience is beneficial for you only if it helps you to live more positively in the present moment. If you make a value judgement on an experience — for example, by placing it in a "bad" box — you are retaining the effects of it in a negative way in your present awareness. If, on the other hand, you see every experience as a learning — or relearning — opportunity, without taking up any other position on it, you are undeviatingly on a secure pathway to the total expression of the free spirit that you are.

How can we make the whole process easier? As I have stressed in earlier sessions, nobody else can take away your negative karma. (For far too long many people in succeeding generations have been suffering under that illusion.) But in acknowledging that the key is

within yourself you don't have to set out on a long trail of penitential exercises or extensive soul searching. You can do that if you
like, of course, and you'll be helped in whatever approach you take.
However, as you know, I'm in favour of simplicity in all things.

In our communication a central challenge is how to overcome the
limitations of your perception as it is within your present human
condition. For that reason in our first book I referred to a belief
which would be familiar to many people of God as a divinity concentrated in three persons — Father, Son and Holy Spirit. I went on
to stress that God cannot be identified in personal terms except in
the sense that God is present in all persons (as well as in all souls
and all life). I thought it might be helpful towards easier understanding to use the symbolism of the Father in terms of those souls who
never lost or who have regained their self-awareness, the Son in
terms of those souls who are still at the start of the journey or who
have not yet mastered the lessons of earth, and the Holy Spirit in
terms of those souls who have evolved beyond the lessons of earth
and who are helping others to find their way — for example, spiritual helpers/guardian angels.

In that symbolism the Father represents the ultimate state of
awareness, with the Son and Holy Spirit, while no less divine, representing interim states. In order to give an idea of relative propor-
tions I subsequently used a measure of 99% to show how many
souls are represented in the symbolism of the Father — with the
proportion continuing to increase according as souls regain their
former state of full awareness.

If I say to you that you are love that's a statement of fact but it
may be difficult for you to see yourself as an individualised entity
within a feeling — something that doesn't appear to have substance.
I have used the symbolism of the Father, etc., in an attempt to
bridge that gap. For example, there are three persons in one God,
those three persons represent all souls, so that all are in one and one
is in all. Each of us exists only because we are animated by, and
linked together in, the loving energy that is God, but it is very
important for us to know that we each have our own unique identi-

ties which will never be merged into an amorphous non-individu-alised mass.

You may remember that at an early stage in our communication I recommended meditation on unity with the Father (in my symbolic usage of that word). I expanded on that suggestion in our third book. I'm coming back to it in this session because, in my view, it's the simplest and best way of all to obtain freedom from negative karmic effects.

In my original suggestion I recommended that you include your guides in the meditation. I have discussed previously a confusion that seems to exist between the notions of guides and higher self (oversoul, in my terminology). If you look to your higher self exclu-sively for guidance you are limiting yourself to the extent that your higher self has not fully regained awareness — you wouldn't be on earth if it had. Equally, as I explained in our first book, your guides, in general, will not have gone beyond the fourth stage of evolution-ary growth, in the context of the seven stages I outlined. While they have access to the totality of consciousness in ways not readily available to you they are still not existing fully in that consciousness because they have chosen to remain at an in-between stage in order to help others to "climb the ladder" of awareness faster — to hold the gate open, as it were, at the fourth stage for others to go through to catch up with them.

I have been hesitant to use the concept 'Father' because of its personalised and, to some, sexist connotation, but it seems warmer than, say, 99%, which sounds rather clinical. Ideally I don't want to use words at all and, in fact, I'm not using words, but my concepts have to be put into words since we have chosen books as our vehi-cles of communication with those who may wish to read them. As far as I am concerned one word is as good as another as long as there is a clear understanding of what is meant — which is that the most evolved possible form of union for you to aspire to is with the Father within the symbolism of that concept as I have outlined it. Your guides are helping you to integrate with your higher self/over-soul and together you expand into a merging with the Father, which involves not alone a linking in consciousness with your guides as oversouls but with all oversouls who have never lost, as well as those who have regained, their awareness. What I'm talking about is the fullness of divine expression without any element of unawareness. It means that you are not uniting yourself with the aspects of soul which are still clouded by negativity as the evolutionary struggle continues. You are in a totally clear space where no vestige of negative influence can intrude.

I have been referring to unity with God/love in other sessions and I don't want to create any misunderstanding between the notions of 'Father' and 'God'; it's too cumbersome and perhaps introduces an unnecessary complication to keep saying 'God, the Father', which is what is really meant. I have described God as the animating force or energy in all life; nothing exists outside of God. The human being who is engaged in what may seem to be the most depraved of activities is as much a part of God as any of the 99%; the all important difference is, of course, that the human has confined his divinity in a prison of unawareness. When you consciously place yourself in union with the Father you are merging with the fully realised divine expression without being affected in any way by the temporary negativity of the balance of the struggling 1%. If the word 'Father' creates any difficulty for you, e.g., because of sexist, religious or personalised overtones, please substitute any word or image that appeals to you as long as you are clear as to what it means to you.

Since nothing exists on earth without somebody having to do something an understandable question for you to ask is — what do you have to do if you wish to act on my suggestion of enabling a feeling of unity with the Father (or whatever concept you prefer)? The last thing I want is that you would get trapped by an image created by a particular word or symbol. I have already referred to the fact that words have to be used in our communication in order to create an understanding between us. Now that we understand each other (I hope!) we can let the definitions go and I'd like to offer in greater detail than I have done previously signposts which I feel can help you reach the desired unity.

1   *You don't have to do anything, as such, other than to allow the feeling to happen.*

2   *As always, the more relaxed you are the better.*

3   *Sit (or stand — whichever suits you) comfortably.*

4   *Invite your guides to help you and join with you in the exercise.*

5   *Don't try to visualise or create anything; if images or words flit across your mind, let them be. Because your intention is clear that you want union with the Father, that has been impressed on your consciousness in a linking with the consciousness of the Father and no effort, other than the intention, is needed on your part.*

6   *Stay with whatever you're feeling. In my view, it's better not to verbalise at all — words are a distraction; but please don't put any pressure on yourself to avoid using words if they keep coming into your head; the main thing is that you don't set up any resistance.*

7   *You don't need to analyse or understand anything or force yourself in any way.*

8   *Surrender completely to your being, Union doesn't have to take any form; it's a feeling which is beyond definition, analysis or thought.*

9   *Thoughts will wander in, of course, as will sounds; just let them be — they will merge into your experience if you don't try to block them out or sit in judgement on them.*

What's new or different about all that and why am I making such a big deal out of it? All your conditioning tends to create complexity. Rituals, rules, regulations, laws, have become endemically human manifestations. What I'm proposing is to get them all out of the way so that there's utter simplicity. Then there's nothing between you and (God) the Father. Then, automatically, all the negative karmic effects fall away from you. And then, of course, you will be free to be truly yourself — your divine self rejoicing in its integration with your temporary humanness.

That's the something more that's demanded now — to let yourself feel your unity with the Father within the symbolic usage of that word as I have endeavoured to express it. In that way you will allow to happen within you a feeling so powerful that all the emotional baggage which you have been carrying will be swept away. As the love of the Father is constantly flowing towards and around every soul in the universe without exception you will also be linking automatically with that flow and thus helping in the best possible way all souls who are still controlled by negative karmic effects.

More dialogue with Shebaka

29th May–13th June: **Patrick Francis** I feel that this is the last book in the series. Is that so?

Shebaka Yes. We have reached the end of our rope, in a manner of speaking, as far as the series is concerned.

PF Does that mean that you won't be communicating with me any more?

S No.

PF Is that all? Let me guess — I'll have to wait and see.

S Well done!

PF If it's okay with you I'd like to do some random exploration with you as well as to bring up questions that often seem to bother people.

S Fine.

PF One of the most common questions goes something like this: how can you say that there's no evil when there are so many examples all through the history of the planet, as we know it, of atrocities committed by some people against others? How can the perpetrators of such atrocities be regarded as divine, part of God? Is that tantamount to saying that God is evil as well as good?

S Those questions, as you know, have figured prominently in our communications, but since they keep coming up it's well to look at them again. In my explanations I have described the states of being as awareness and different degrees of non-awareness. In ultimate awareness souls are expressing their divinity fully. Until they reach that state they continue to cloak their divinity in expressions of non-awareness.

It's difficult for people not to take up positions in the immediacy of whatever presents itself to them. Of course I can't deny the awfulness of some of the things that people have done, and do, to each other as adults and to children and animals. When these actions are considered in isolation they can only be regarded as evil and the perpetrators similarly so. But in spiritual terms nothing can be viewed in an isolationist context.

It's always easier to explain something by using a hypothetical example.

From an early age Philip got involved in criminal activities, such as mugging, robbery. As he grew into adulthood he had increasingly less compunction about injuring, sometimes severely, helpless people. It didn't bother him that from time to time he was apprehended and sentenced to terms of imprisonment. On release he resumed his criminal career with renewed vigour and cruelty, showing no vestige of compassion for any of his victims, whatever their circumstances.

However, in midlife Philip was involved in a serious accident which left him completely immobilised for several months. Initially he was hospitalised and later he was taken care of by family members from whom he had earlier separated himself. During his convalescence a transformation took place in him. The kindness shown to him by people for whom the question — "what's in it for me?" — had obviously no meaning slowly began to make an impression on him. Feelings which he had hitherto suppressed started to surface in him. Suddenly people had individual identities rather than being regarded as potential victims. It nonplussed him that it didn't seem to matter to the people around him that he had a reputation as a dangerous criminal. They treated him no differently from anybody else and even, unbelievably, with affection, although all that was hard for him to accept initially.

To cut a long story short, the outcome was that Philip decided to train as a physical therapist and has gone on to do wonderful healing work with people. He has become as dedicated in his new life as he had previously been in his old one.

Let's look at this case study in a two-fold way.

If we take Philip himself first I think it's easy to accept that he's not an evil man even though many people would have categorised him as such on the evidence of his criminal activities. In familiar human terminology it might be said that the capacity for evil in him has been transformed into the capacity for good.

That still leaves us with his earlier actions which injuriously affected the lives of many people. How can they be regarded as other than evil? On one level, which is the immediate human one, they can't. But in spiritual terms there's always a broader perspective. I can't consider any question or any case without taking into account the continuity of soul, which means that whatever happens to any individual needs to be put into the context of that individual's journey as a soul. Put in that light it may well be that what would be regarded in its immediacy as evil would, in fact, be ultimately positive in its effects.

May I remind you that humanity is a temporary condition and that its purpose is to enable growth in awareness. At the risk of boring you I must repeat that all happenings are only important in the effects they create; and those effects can only be judged within the broad canvas of each individual's evolution.

It's important to mention, too, that some souls have chosen human manifestation in catalytic roles, and that's likely to be a continuing feature of human evolution as long as it's considered desirable. In that context the easier role is, you'll agree, that which is generally seen in a positive or often saintly light. But what of the soul who, in a human role, has elected to become the subject of public opprobrium for the purpose of acting as an agent of change in people's attitudes? There have been several such souls in human history who have been held up as symbols of infamy and evil but who in the process have influenced people towards looking into themselves and how they behave towards others. They are the unsung heroic beings. It's easy, for instance, to perform such a role in a play or a movie, where everybody knows that it's not "real life", but it's a different story when one doesn't have that cover.

A classic example is the role of Judas in the story of Jesus. Had it not been for the part played by Judas, whose name subsequently became synonymous with betrayal, the story could not have been recorded as it was. Was Judas evil, do you think? Were his actions evil? I hope you see that when the perspective is broadened there are no facile judgements or categorisations.

In Philip's case the transformation took place within his present lifetime. It's a fact,of course, that in many cases no such transformation has yet taken place even after many physical lives; but it will, because each soul's divine nature cannot be suppressed indefinitely.

You may remember that in an earlier session (incidentally on God, in our third book) I used an analogy of the soul as an electric light bulb which, though switched on, is buried in earth and doesn't show any light. When the earth is removed from it the bulb shows all its light. It's the same bulb all the time. That's the process of evolution in a nutshell. The light is the divinity which is always there even when it's hidden. What you call evil is the earth of unawareness which ultimately falls away and the divine reality is then revealed in all its glory. The love that God is never rejects or abandons or separates itself from any soul; the soul itself is responsible for its separation.

PF It seems that there's still a big gap in perceptiveness between our worlds. Is it possible to be more specific as to how the gap can be narrowed?

S That very perceptiveness doesn't allow me to be more specific than I have been. The human being is always looking for chapter and verse, for the maps that will pinpoint his direction for him in fine detail. That's not the way of spirit. In our sessions I have attempted to paint a broad picture of life in spirit in the hope that

that will help those who will have access to our books — or who already have had such access — to integrate more fully their divinity with their humanness. Thus — that is, as that integration happens — the gap will be closed.

PF What, in your view, is the biggest single challenge facing humanity at present?

S Facetiously, I might say not to ask questions like that! Seriously, though, I'd like to put the question another way: what's the biggest single challenge facing each human being at present? My answer, predictably I suppose, is to attain freedom from all negative karmic effects through union with (God) the Father along the lines we discussed in the last chapter and earlier ones. Humanity as a global concept takes its significance from the individuals who comprise it. As each individual finds inner completeness and peace the problems of humanity will be proportionately diminished. No revolution, no organisation, no religion, no system, will provide adequate solutions, as should be obvious at this stage of evolution. Global or generic answers could only be effective if people were to be standardised, like robots. That's why utopia, as I have described it, will have no prescribed formulas.

PF That's why too, partly at least I think, you don't favour gurus?

S It depends on what's meant by gurus. While it's true that each soul ultimately has to find — or rediscover — its own truth, the help that's available through the interlinking of consciousness in all souls is a hugely significant factor in growth of awareness. Because souls are at different levels of awareness those at lower levels have much to gain from interaction with those at higher levels.

Difficulties have arisen in the human evolution when some people have set themselves up, or have been set up, as the custodians of absolute truth and have dogmatically declared that the way to salvation is only possible through faithful adherence to that "truth". Sadly, such absolutism has attracted millions of devotees throughout human history and has led to all sorts of fanatical excesses. Any belief or practice which inhibits people's free will or seeks to impose itself on them or control them through confining them within behavioural prescriptions is spiritually damaging.

But, of course, there are teachers and pupils and there will continue to be a need for teachers for as long as the need for the human condition exists. In our previous dialogue I have stressed the all important role of education — in a vastly more extended and individually oriented format than it exists at present — in solving the problems of the world. The role of the teacher — or guru — is ideally that of a facilitator who provides a platform through which pupils will find their individually unique ways and truths which may or may not be similar to those of the teacher.

So, to answer your question, if the word "guru" can be taken to mean an empowering teacher rather than somebody who seeks to attract devotees I have no difficulty with it.

PF Even when one accepts unreservedly how significant spiritually is non-interference with free will it's still very difficult to see how that can be put into practice fully in the human state. We came up against this dilemma (to me) in our previous dialogue in discussing criminal activities and responses to them.

S I understand. But there is free will or there isn't. Once you accept that each soul (whether in spirit or temporary human manifestation) has free will, it follows that any enforced restriction of that, whether by a system or by an individual, has damaging spiritual effects on both parties. If you start bringing in qualifying considerations, such as, "I agree with the notion of free will in principle, but in practice it has to be subordinated to the common good" or "Free will is a great thing but you have to draw the line somewhere" or "Nobody has the right to do wrong", you're now subject to the vagaries of changing perceptions of "common good" or "right" or "wrong" and to the potential for abuse inherent in those perceptions, such as those promulgated by self proclaimed representatives of all "right thinking people" — whoever they may be!

PF Recently I heard about a 'Shabaka stone' in the British Museum, and subsequently I read that this stone relates to a King

Shabaka who reigned in Egypt from 712 to 698 BC, and who, having discovered that material on which the story of creation according to the god Ptah had been written had been partially destroyed by worms, arranged that the surviving part of it should be carved in stone in order to preserve it — hence the Shabaka stone. Although the spelling of the name is slightly different (Shab instead of Sheb) from that used in our books, was that you in one of your incarnations?

S Yes, it was. I thought it important that the material, such as it was in its extant form, should be available for future generations. Let's hope that the record of our communications will prove to be more durable! Incidentally isn't there a neat symbolic irony about some of the material having been eaten by worms?

I chose to use that name in our communications because it seemed to me to have an appropriateness in the context of what we were endeavouring to achieve. I didn't reveal the historical connection to you at the outset because it would have personalised (or humanised!) me too much as far as you were concerned. Isn't that so?

PF Yes. I found it helpful initially that the name had no associations for me. I didn't attempt to put a shape on you or to identify you in terms of gender.

Since our communication has been a two-way process, which for its clarity and accuracy has been dependent on my use of words, I'd like to check with you again at this stage whether the books are a true record of all the material conveyed by you.

S Words are a form of structure. Human affairs are ordered through structure. Communication in the human state relies to a large extent on the structure of language. It is extremely difficult to convey the notion of spirituality in terms of structure since it doesn't know structure. The challenge for us was to provide an understanding of spirituality in a way that would be humanly comprehensible. In so far as words could do that, I'm happy that the books convey accurately the substance of my communications.

PF I know that in some of our sessions you have outlined in quite a lot of detail what life in spirit is like and the reasons why it's not desirable that communication between the spirit and physical states should be generally evidentially obvious. In my own case, as you well know, I have from time to time pleaded for more clear indications that I was connecting with you rather than talking to myself. Because the material in the communications made so much sense to me the need for more obvious proof of your existence diminished — it kept rearing its head occasionally — and, as you said, even if I could get all sorts of physical proof, that wouldn't be of any use to anybody else in so far as acceptance of the material was concerned. So I settled on trust and I'm (usually!) happy with that.

When I move off this "mortal coil", though, suppose I want to have a chat with you, how can that be arranged?

S Exactly as it is now; just send a thought to me and, hey presto!, here I am or there I am, whatever you like.

PF But how different will it be? For example, I'll be able to see you, won't I? What will you look like? And what will I look like?

S Yes, you'll be able to see me.

When the human state was designed the physical framework was based on how souls appear to each other in spirit. There are no deformities, of course; they (the deformities) evolved in physical appearance for various reasons which I have explored in previous sessions.

Souls may choose to manifest as male or female, whichever they wish. As I have already explained, when souls progress beyond the third stage of evolutionary growth (as I outlined the stages in our first book) gender distinction doesn't apply, but some souls like to regard themselves as female and others as male. It all makes for variety.

In whatever way a soul chooses to manifest, once it progresses beyond the third stage it will always be radiant and beautiful. And, needless to say, there's no ageing.

PF Perhaps you would elaborate a little on that.

As I understand the reincarnational process, in physical lifetimes the choice of gender is governed or, at least, influenced by a soul's purpose in a particular lifetime. I gather from what you're saying that that process continues, although obviously in a different way, in the spirit state?

S As you know, the physical state is intended as a platform for transformation, with the objective of balancing feelings and thoughts and allowing a soul's divinity to express itself, or, put another way, releasing all negative karmic effects. Because of the ways in which male and female roles evolved in the expression of free will it usually transpired that the balance could potentially be more easily attained through diversification between the gender manifestations.

The situation is broadly the same at the second and third stages in spirit.

Once a soul moves into the fourth stage and beyond that the balance is already there so that then a soul's choice is usually based on whatever sort of continuing expression it would like to have.

I know that there are all sorts of tensions — as well as intimately loving bonds — between the sexes and that marriage and similar types of relationship are often beset by intense conflicts — but again all that is a consequence of how free will has been exercised in human evolution. Whatever about the tensions, it's nice, isn't it?, that there are the two sexes, even for those who have chosen to express themselves in intimate relationship with the same gender as themselves.

PF It's probably a stupid question, but are you glad that you won't be experiencing the human state again?

S At least you didn't ask me to agree that it's a stupid question. No doubt you wouldn't expect me to be judgemental!

Yes, I am glad.

However, I want to add that the potential for happiness in the physical world is enormous and is realisable; not alone that, but I'm certain that, as I set out in some detail in our last book, the planet is evolving towards its paradisal expression.

PF Will it continue to exist, then, indefinitely?

S Not as you know it. It will go through much transformation and will become what I have chosen to call utopia because of the meaning associated with that word. All that's a long way off, unfortunately, but the good news is that it's already set on its course.

PF In the introduction to the first book you outlined briefly the background to how you came to be communicating with me. Since you could see broadly how things were going to evolve, was it part of your design, if I may use that word, that whether the book was published or not was so finely balanced?

S As I had explained, before you incarnated we had made an arrangement that we would cooperate in the recording of the material contained in the books. But that arrangement was always subject to how you would exercise your free will. I have to admit, though, that there wasn't ever really any doubt about that.

It was understandable that once you had decided to take the plunge and allow the first book to be published you would assume that everything would be plain sailing. But it was very important, which I know you quickly came to realise, that our enterprise would not be exempt from human experience generally. Because you were required to be patient and to trust and the books became, in a sense, a monument to that trust, it was much easier for you to accept and validate that what was being suggested to our readers about letting go and trusting, etc., was not in any way misleading them; your own experience of the process was tangible proof that it works.

PF I want to bring up just one other matter with you to do with the fact that in recent years as part of the new wave of consciousness established structures, particularly religious ones, have been breaking down and for many people they are no longer the symbols of security they once were. In my experience many people are finding it difficult to manage without the 'maps' that were previously available and acceptable to them even in their paternalistic wrapping. I know that over and over again you have reminded us of the help that's available to us, if we're prepared to receive it, as we struggle along our individual paths, but still there can be a somewhat overwhelming sense of isolation sometimes. Since we have come to the end of the series I couldn't resist the temptation to ask you whether you'd like to say anything more about all that.

S I sympathise with people who are feeling temporarily marooned. There's security — of a kind — in being given a set of rules and promised that if you obey them you'll be rewarded with eternal happiness in a specific location (heaven). When the rules are removed and you're informed that there's no location, as such, what can you hold on to? Solidity has disappeared into formlessness.

The whole point is, of course, that letting go of all the peripheral frameworks brings one face to face with oneself. As it's a fact that you're unique, as each individual is, and that's something that's beyond question — you know that there's nobody in existence who is exactly the same as you — how can you fit into a common mould? Isn't it a fair assumption that no matter how much you might admire — or even envy — another or others you wouldn't want to be anybody else?

What more can I say to you now than I have already said? Please enjoy the wonder of being unique and yet always linked to the loving energy (God) that animates the whole universe. How could you ever be yourself if you had to live eternally within a prescribed set of rules? What could be more marvellous than that you have in store for you the freedom of the whole universe, with nobody to say to you that you shouldn't be this or you shouldn't do that, that however you are and in whatever way you want to express yourself is entirely a matter for yourself and that you can share yourself and your joy in life with whomsoever you wish?

Maybe you're in an interim state which is at times somewhat confusing and things get on top of you sometimes. But don't forget that there's always somebody to hold your hand, not to walk for you but to help you to walk. You're free to create your own map — and it will be a masterpiece, have no doubt of that. And it won't be like any map you've ever seen or known because it will have no boundaries and no fixed coordinating points.

Au revoir

20th–26th June: In case there's any misunderstanding — as so often happens with words — I want to mention that I meant my concluding comments in the last dialogue to apply to everybody. That mightn't have been quite clear because we had been mixing the general and the particular in the session.

When I say 'you' in this the concluding instalment in the series I mean it in a general way, too.

It sounds so final when we talk about coming to the end of something. In the physical sense you are conditioned to endings. For example, it's normal for you to talk of projects as being unfinished — whatever that might mean! One of the reasons for presenting these communications in a series of volumes was to create a feeling of continuity. And while it seems appropriate now to leave the words as they are contained within the covers of five books, I hope that you will take it for granted that the continuity of our communication will not be broken. You may like to know that whenever you dip into any of the books, even if only for a few moments, you are connecting with me if you wish to do so. That doesn't mean that I'm seeking to intrude in any way on your relationship with your guides and/or your oversoul. We operate in harmony with each other — as I'm sure you'd expect.

Never before in the history of the planet have so many people's energies been focused on peace — with the infinite support of all of us in spirit who are similarly motivated. You have no idea of the power that's generated by the energy emanating from even one person; please don't undervalue how important your contribution is. It doesn't matter whether you are in a central position of obvious influence or in what may seem like an obscure backwater. When your starting point is finding peace within yourself and when you link with all the evolved loving energy of the universe, whether along the lines of my earlier suggestions or in whatever way feels best to you, the effect is astronomical. It's difficult for you to conceive of that because you have no obvious evidence to confirm it for you, so for the present I hope you'll be prepared to accept my assurance that it is so.

In the communications which form the substance of the five books I have endeavoured to provide facts and concepts and suggestions with the object of giving you a greater understanding of the whole scheme of life and ways of finding ever increasing fulfilment and happiness in your own expression.

Needless to say, I make no demands on your acceptance of the material in the communications; it would be highly presumptuous and interfering of me to do so. Above all, I hope that our journey together to this stage will have been helpful for you in finding your way and your truth.

I appreciate very much your patience and your trust. It has been — is, I should say, — a great joy and privilege for me to have the honour of being with you in such an intimate way. My love and best wishes are with you always.